ANCESTRAL LANGUAGE ACQUISITION AMONG NATIVE AMERICANS

A Study of a Haida Language Class

ANCESTRAL LANGUAGE ACQUISITION AMONG NATIVE AMERICANS
A Study of a Haida Language Class

Frederick H. White

With a Preface by
John H. Peacock

The Edwin Mellen Press
Lewiston•Queenston•Lampeter

Library of Congress Cataloging-in-Publication Data

White, Frederick H.
   Ancestral language acquisition among Native Americans: a study of a Haida language class / Frederick H. White ; with a preface by John H. Peacock.
      p. cm.
   Includes bibliographical references and index.
   ISBN-13: 978-0-7734-5064-6
   ISBN-10: 0-7734-5064-5
   I. Title.

hors série.

A CIP catalog record for this book is available from the British Library.

The Edwin Mellen Press
Box 450
Lewiston, New York
USA 14092-0450

The Edwin Mellen Press
Box 67
Queenston, Ontario
CANADA L0S 1L0

The Edwin Mellen Press, Ltd.
Lampeter, Ceredigion, Wales
UNITED KINGDOM SA48 8LT

Printed in the United States of America

Dedication

To my parents

I would like to thank my parents Edmund and Margaret Bernhard for all their support and encouragement; they have given me life.

Table of Contents

Preface

I know Professor Frederick White from the Division of Native American Literatures session he's organized for years at the annual convention of the 30,000 member Modern Language Association of college and university professors. Among more than 760 sessions, White's is the only one on Native American languages. The 2005 session spawned an ad hoc subcommittee of Lakota, Dakota, Oneida, Miami, and Haida members who produced a statement approved by the MLA Executive Council urging colleges and universities to work with Native American language communities to update dictionaries, grammars, orthographies, curricula, and other materials for teaching Native American languages in colleges and universities.

This book is about how younger students' cultural differences affect their second language learning of ancestral tribal languages. After presenting evidence that Haida first graders really do learn and participate differently than their Euro-Canadian peers, White considers how these differences might be accommodated to help all children learn better.

Paralleling early education research done on the Wasco and Paiute confederated tribes of Oregon's Warm Springs Reservation, White found that Haida first graders in the Massett Haida tribal school tend not to compete academically. Expecting them to only alienates them not only from American mainstream culture but from their own Haida traditions, in which appearing to outsmart others is culturally unacceptable, the model learner being first an observer/apprentice and only later a participant. Also paralleling Warm Springs research, White observed that Haida children respond to teachers' questions less but visit with each other and wander in and out of class more than mainstream students. This may be, White suggests, because at tribal gatherings where attention shifts among as many speakers as in a normal class, nobody equivalent to a teacher formally decides who gets to talk and when, and children are free to come and go and interact with whomever they please while others talk. Euro-American first graders transition easier from informal kinship gatherings to classrooms controlled by non-kin authority figures with whom they have already had more experience than Haida children. The latter do better with a teacher they are allowed to call "auntie" or "grandma," but even then, rather than raise hands to talk to her, they tend to get out of their seats to go ask her something, often out of hearing of the others. Non-Indian first graders in the Haida class raise their hands more, even though of course they too get to call Haida teachers grandma or auntie, and, according to parents, cherish these women.

Could it be that not just Haidas but all first graders might benefit as well from being allowed to wait to participate until they are good and ready, that all might do better in more cooperative first grade classrooms? If so, then ascertaining and acknowledging as much would only make arguments for such classrooms stronger.

As for how teachers shape student behavior, White cites research on an Odawa teacher who gives students three times longer to answer than a Euro-Canadian teacher does. In turn he finds Haida teachers differ from mainstream ones in how much and what kind of participation they expect and therefore require of Haida students -- subtle differences that have received little attention. When "peripheral participation" – neither fruitless nor pressured – is encouraged at the students' discretion, Haida first graders participate more. Typically they are silent or give wrong (because premature) answers when forced to demonstrate skills or knowledge beyond what their community would normally expect of a nonparticipating observer/apprentice; or else they deliberately give incorrect answers or shrug their shoulders so as to compel the teacher to ask someone else for the correct one. By not forcing these kinds of participation, Haida teachers take the stress off and free Haida students to participate more, when they are ready. Doing this in Haida language classes where participation is crucial allows students to concentrate on rather than anxiously filter out the language. By contrast, mainstream teachers actually ratchet up the stress level by quickly stifling student interactions not directly related to instruction, thus maintaining the teacher's own sole authority over who speaks when. Tolerant of much more noise and interruption, Haida teachers let students wander or speak when they want.

Reading White's discussion of competition, I remembered my half-blood Dakota mother's taking me aside as a child to remind me that the A's I received in school did not make me smarter than my brothers. White's research on classroom dynamics helped me make sense of Dakota language and culture classes I have taken, observed, or team-taught as an adult. I remember a young woman wandering in late to a tribal college class, going right up to the instructor's desk in the middle of his lesson, asking him to fill out some forms, leaving, and coming back later to ask if he had completed them – something he didn't seem to mind, but which I found outrageous until I read this book. Even though he told students at my guest lecture that I had studied and taught in Euro-American universities and therefore expected them to ask and respond to probing questions, many more students came up to me individually afterwards than responded during class. My twenty-two year old white nephew was taken aback by the way some of his students would only occasionally come to his film making class at the tribal college, even though they all seemed to relish the group projects. The instructor of a multigenerational Dakota class I took at a reservation community school seemed to tolerate a level of absenteeism and tardiness that until I read this book I was amazed did not undermine the class. On the contrary, when she herself was not there, students would come anyway and engage in group activities that "auntie" or "grandma," as she was called, had introduced, such as playing scrapple in Dakota. When I joined the class, she said I could be another "uncle" to several toddlers who came with young single mothers and expected to sit on the laps of older adults. White's point that Haida teachers themselves were more physical with their students than were non-Indian teachers in this litigious age reminded me of a male Dakota teacher whom I saw a little boy approach and lean into for an affectionate hug. So different was this from anything I had ever seen in my son's white schools that I had assumed it was unusual in tribal schools, too. Evidently it is not.

Besides enlightening me about classroom practices that I had misunderstood, White's observations of non-Indian teachers having distracting conversations while Haida teachers were in their classrooms trying to teach their students confirmed what I've witnessed on my reservation, where non-Indian English teachers don't have to be recertified as often as the senior Dakota teacher by the board of education, none of whose members know the language they are certifying her to teach.

Without collegial respect and administrative support, Native language teachers cannot overcome curricular neglect of their languages. White calculates that only 24 hours per year, 168 total for K-7 are devoted to Haida instruction. To achieve the stated purpose of producing fluent speakers requires 600-700 contact hours of exposure, according to Arapaho and Hawaiian immersion data. At the rate of just two weekly lessons for an average of 15 minutes daily of actual language instruction, it would take 13 years to achieve the minimum 600 hours needed for fluency. Also insufficient (though necessary) to produce fluency is vocabulary memorization, which White implies is the main curricular model he observed. Phrases need to be produced from memorized vocabulary, and sentences and discourse from phrases. The bottom line, White concludes, is that the best lessons will be in vain if Haida students don't participate more than they currently do, and the contribution of his findings is to suggest they will participate more if their different learning and participation styles are accommodated.

Far fewer Native Americans were defeated on 19th-century battlefields than in 19th- and 20th- century Indian boarding schools which prohibited "primitive" languages, "savage" ceremonies, and clan based social systems that promoted communal sharing over individualistic striving. After generations of education for extinction no wonder so many Indians still distrust impersonal school authority. To reverse this terrible and continuing toll requires an embrace of cooperative learning on non-Indian terms. Respect must replace disregard for the deep roots of this kind of learning in tribal cultures with extended family systems in which authority figures are looked to as guides by apprentice learners who tend to listen, observe, and collaborate rather than single themselves out for individual recognition in accordance with the mainstream ethos of personal autonomy. Tribal teaching and learning traditions will be appreciated only by mainstream educators who no longer take their own pedagogies for granted as universal. This book will open the eyes of Indian and non-Indian educators alike.

John Peacock

John Peacock is Professor of Language, Literature, and Culture at Maryland Institute College of Art, Baltimore, author of numerous articles in Native American Studies, Composition Studies, Cultural Studies, Religious Studies, and creative writing in poetry and short stories.

LIST OF SYMBOLS

CONSONANTS

b	voiced bilabial stop
p	voiceless bilabial stop
m	bilabial nasal stop
d	voiced alveolar stop
t	voiceless alveolar stop
t'	glottalized *t*
n	alveolar nasal stop
j	voiced (alveo) palatal affricate
ts	voiceless (alveo) palatal affricate
ts'	glottalized *ts*
s	voiceless alveolar fricative
dl	voiced lateral affricate
hl	voiceless lateral fricative
tl	voiceless alveolar affricate
tl'	glottalized *tl*
l	voiced alveolar lateral
g	voiced velar stop
k	voiceless velar stop
k'	glottalized *k*
ng	voiced velar nasal stop
r	voiced uvular fricative
ꝁ	voiceless uvular stop
ꝁ'	glottalized uvular stop
x	voiceless velar fricative
7	glottal stop, (used only initially)
'	glottal stop, (used only medially)

h	voiceless glottal fricative
y	palatal glide
w	labiovelar glide

VOWELS

a	low unrounded vowel
aa	same as above but lengthened
ay	mid front unrounded vowel
i	high front unrounded vowel
ii	same as above but lengthened
u	high back rounded vowel
uu	same as above but lengthened
o	mid back rounded vowel

ACKNOWLEDGEMENTS

First, I want to thank Haida Gwaii School District # 50 for allowing me to pursue this research. I offer special thanks for "Dora" and "Genie" without whose cooperation none of this research could have been possible. I want to thank my dissertation committee, co-chairs Marianne Celce-Murcia and Paul Kroskrity, as well as Pam Munro and Duane Champagne because they inspired, challenged, and guided me so graciously through each phase of the writing. I also want to thank Old Masset Band Council for their support of my educational pursuits. Finally, I want to thank my wife, Teresa, who had to be patient with me as I traveled to and fro gathering information, presenting at conferences, and writing and revising this book. *Demaanuu haaw'aa.*

1

Chapter 1
Introduction

Reversing language shift and language loss are crucial issues in many Native American communities. In Canada, First Nations (the Canadian term for 'Native American') communities currently experience critical shift and loss. The 1991 census in Canada reports disturbingly low numbers of fluent ancestral language speakers (Report of the Assembly of First Nations language and literacy secretariat 1992). Historically, cultural opposition, enforced assimilation, government exploitation, and missionization succeeded in reducing the use of many Native American languages. These efforts not only strove to eliminate Native American languages, but the culture of their speakers as well. The main tool used in reducing and eliminating ancestral language use was formal education within a strict English only setting (Report of the Assembly of First Nations language and literacy secretariat 1992:20). The residential schools' legacy encompasses not only the transition to a formal education setting, but the systematic eradication of the culture of each First Nations student.

Only within the last quarter of the twentieth century has the Canadian government implemented efforts to address the problem of reversing language shift among its First Nations people. Currently, the problem for the majority of the First Nations communities across Canada is the absence of any speakers acquiring the ancestral language as a mother tongue (Fourth report of the standing committee on aboriginal affairs 1990:18). Lack of community efforts exacerbates the problem, and more often than not the main effort of salvaging Native American languages falls on the local school board. The result is that many Native American students now learn or study their ancestral language only as a second language within a school context. Ancestral language learning as a means to reverse language shift has thus become a field ripe for research.

In this book, I am particularly interested in addressing the issues of reversing language shift and recovering language loss as it concerns the Haida in British Columbia. The Haida have lived on Haida Gwaii (formerly known as the Queen Charlotte Islands) for the last nine millennia, according to the curator of Canada's National Museum (Johnson 1987). Only within the last 100 years has another language (i.e., English) infiltrated the islands and replaced Haida as the language of wider communication on Haida Gwaii. This language shift process, occurring mainly within the twentieth century, has numerous explanations: greater foreign contact at the end of the Nineteenth Century, including trade and missionary endeavors; foreign colonization of Haida Gwaii, and greater governmental interactions on the islands involving the process of territorial expansion and community development. I will address the language loss and language shift issues specifically in terms of education.

Formal education has tremendously impacted both language shift and loss in Canada (Royal Commission on Aboriginal Peoples, 1996). Governmentally sanctioned and often assisted by missionary efforts, the process of formal education for the Haida began at the dawn of the Twentieth Century. The realities of transitioning to English and then to the formal school-based mode of education included forced departure of Haidas from their communities and often required their rejection of their native culture as well (see Achneepineskum 1993; Collison 1993). Perhaps the two most difficult aspects were the enforced transition to a strict English only environment and being in a western classroom. The boarding schools' prohibition on the use of all languages other than English made speaking native languages a punishable offense. Thus, historically, the transition to English represented a painful loss of both Haida language and culture.

Within the last two decades, Canadian governmental intervention, through education once again, has attempted to reverse the language loss among First Nations communities. As a result of government funding, First Nations language programs were initiated all across Canada. On Haida Gwaii, the Haida language program began in the late 1980's.

It is within this environment of government intervention and the school-based attempts at reversing language shift that I began my involvement with Haida students learning Haida as a second language. My interest piqued when I began to consider the implications of Susan Philips' works, "Participant structures and communicative competence: Warm Springs children in community and classroom"(1972a), and *The invisible culture: Communication in classroom and community on the Warm Springs Indian reservation* (1983). I saw parallels between the Haida and the Warm Springs Indian communities that I thought were worthy of research.

Using Philips' premise concerning Native American student behavior, that the Warm Springs Indian students participated in the classroom very differently from their non-Indian classmates, I consider in this book the language learning process in a Haida classroom. In particular, I look at Haida student classroom behavior to assess implications of their learning Haida as a second language in the context of their own participation style.

Formal and informal education among Native Americans.

Each culture has priorities and peculiarities about what children should learn, and, perhaps most importantly, how and why they should learn them. Each culture also has different modes of attaining such knowledge. For most cultures in North America, the process was generally informal, daily, and noncompetitive. That setting would change drastically as a result of colonization. Eventually, with the expansion of the Canadian and U.S. governments, the process of education changed radically. I want to reflect on three aspects of indigenous student participation in three educational settings:

    1.   The traditional setting which included daily life and experiences prior to contact. This setting, based largely on

kinship structure for learning, included the learners' community and environment.

2. The transition to the formal school setting which included discarding of the prior setting for a classroom. This transitional setting represents diffusion of the Haidas' linguistic and socio-cultural heritage as well as systematic assimilationist efforts.

3. The current school system setting in which all students find themselves, even on the reservations.

For each of these learning settings, I examine the basis for learning and consider the transition to the latter two settings. The result provides the groundwork for my looking at the Haida data in a contextual ethnography of the classroom.

Traditional education setting.

Life was different for Native Americans prior to western contact. The pace of life was set by priorities of the seasons. Learning was daily and unscheduled, but most importantly, learning was kinship based. The transition from an informal kinship educational setting to a formal educational setting was not easy and still is not easy for both educators and students (see Reyner 1981:20; Sindell 1974:340). The informal style of learning prior to contact with Europeans included intimate kinship involvement on a daily basis. The most important aspect of the kinship transmission of knowledge, customs, and history included the setting of such learning, the learning environment and the content, which were practical or historical. Most often both were blended in the process of survival (Armstrong 1987; Marashio 1982:2). Such learning was not limited to one location in a building for six hours a day; rather, it was a daily process which included specific locations within the Haida/Native American environment.

For many Native Americans, daily life was a process of learning with the ultimate purpose of preparing children to be functional members of their community (Tafoya 1989:40). The children learned their roles, their societal responsibilities, survival skills, artistic skills, such as carving and weaving, their histories, and tribal stories, all of which they themselves would, after the completion of their apprenticeship, pass on as they became parents and elders themselves (Stairs 1993: 87). The oral tradition, the most dominant cultural tradition among Native North American communities, instilled children with tribal histories and stories in both community dwelling places and natural settings. Much of the apprenticeship, especially concerning survival skills, involved the Haida in learning about their environment, and therefore both boys and girls received most of their practical learning out in the open air, in the forests, on the beaches, and wherever they needed to be to learn a particular skill being taught (see Blackman 1982:79; Friesen, Archibald, & Jack 1992).

One important aspect of this informal learning environment concerns the content and the "teachers". The main teachers were usually family members, and the content had a functional purpose to ensure survival and to preserve the tribe's oral history through stories and songs. The cultural knowledge needed could be separated into two categories, gender specific and gender neutral. Much of the knowledge that needed to be learned was gender specific, and as such, the teacher was appropriately of the same gender as the learner (Report of the Assembly of First Nations language and literacy secretariat 1992:40). Thus, for the girls, it was usually the mother, an older sister, an aunt, or even the grandmother (Blackman 1982:92) who played the most important role in most Native American societies. For the boys, along with the father, the mother's brothers and the mother's father taught the youths the most important things in life. The kinship system was the foundation of the community, particularly with respect to bringing the novice learner through each stage of learning.

The stages of learning in this informal setting often provided children with a very exclusive relationship with their teacher. Most often, the setting was one-on-one with a particular kin, and the process included participation at the discretion of the learner. It was mainly through repeated observation that the learners gained enough confidence to venture participation. When the learner was confident, he or she actively participated. The student was in no way pressured to learn things at a given pace (see Friesen, Archibald, & Jack 1992:58-9).

These factors, the kinship apprenticeship model, the educational content, the location, and the participatory style of learning would greatly conflict with the formal education process introduced with the transition to the western style of schooling.

Transition to formal education.

The dates at which formal education was introduced vary from tribe to tribe regarding the process of educational transition, but concerted efforts in Canada began about the last quarter of the nineteenth century (Armitage 1995:79). Formal education has been a problematic issue for Native Americans since they began going to school. The transition from the informal, natural, kinship setting to the formal, isolated, authoritarian setting was not easy, and even now presents a challenge for educators (Whyte 1986). The most important elements to consider in the transition phase to the formal setting are:

1. The location of learning
2. The purpose of education
3. The content of the instruction
4. The formal style of education

These four elements present a foundation for understanding my final section concerning participation because it is important to consider precursors of these elements in light of current participation patterns.

The first element of the transition to formal education was most notably the location. No longer was it the land, the oceans, rivers, mountains, fields; rather, it was a schoolhouse. A room enclosed with four walls and perhaps a window or two became the exclusive site for twelve years of learning. There are exceptions, such as the Tewa and their kiva, and the long house for some Eastern tribes though in both cases, the locations/buildings were not exclusive locations for learning, and in both situations, these locations were there previous to schools and continued after. This transition to a single location would be unremarkable if it were some place near the students' home community, but history presents us with different facts. The students were often forcibly removed from their communities and taken to residential schools hundreds of miles from their homes (see Friesen, Archibald, & Jack 1992:60-4). Being unable to return home and the lack of family nearby resulted in psychological trauma that some students struggle to express to this day (see Achneepineskum 1993 and Collison 1993). The shift from natural settings to the classroom was drastic even when it was voluntary, let alone when it was forced.

Intricately tied to the location of formal education were the initial educational goals or purposes. Historically, there are two main sources of efforts to educate Native Americans. First was the missionary presence, whose emphasis on the Gospel motivated instruction as well as the basics of reading and writing. Often the message of the Gospel included forsaking all of the students' culture, including language, because their culture represented a state of "fallenness" which required rejection (Friesen, Archibald, & Jack 1992:60; Kwan 1998; Report of the Assembly of First Nations language and literacy secretariat 1992:69). The other aspect was governmental efforts which implemented vigorous assimilative programs in order to prepare Native American students to become members of Canadian or American society with as few vestiges of their culture as possible (Royal Commission on Aboriginal Peoples 1996:13). In time, the two efforts would join together with the ultimate purpose of assimilating the students to their new life in their new society. One main target for assimilation was language, resulting in a strict English only policy rigidly enforced upon the students. With the advent of English only, and especially the loss of the students' ancestral language, it was assumed that acclimating them to the newer culture would be much easier.

The strict English only policy served as the basis not only for educational goals, but for content as well. The assimilative purpose included curriculum content that tried to instill new values and a new outlook in life, one that incorporated values different from those of the students' home community. The "three Rs: reading, 'riting, and 'rithmetic" (i.e., reading, writing, and arithmetic), focused on skills not necessarily needed within the home communities. For example, math skills of division and multiplication usually had no practical application on most reserves or reservations (Report of the Assembly of First Nations language and literacy secretariat 1992:14-15). But perhaps the greatest impact came from the reading content, especially the subject of history, because the starting point for local history was 1492 and in many cases still is. The new history classes often disregarded (at best, and most often degraded) any tribal accounts of history. Again, intricately tied with the educational goals, the content reflected the assimilationist efforts to eliminate the students' cultural ties to their home communities (Fourth report of the standing committee on aboriginal affairs 1990:14).

Finally, the transition to this style of education represented one of the greatest educational constraints. The learning environment became a very restricted location, the classroom. The setting in which children learned prior to coming to the classroom was informal, seasonal, and kinship oriented. Formal classroom learning required attention to one person, the teacher, and the teacher was in control of everything that went on in the classroom. I will explore this in more detail in the section on participation, but suffice it to say here that the structure for learning became formal, rigid and authoritarian in style, with the students having little or no social contact with the teacher.

These four aspects provide the context for comparison of current participation and also provide a context for understanding the current educational situation. Given the focus of this book, knowing this history illuminates understanding of the present.

9

Current classroom participation setting

The literature on Native American student educational participation is vast. Of particular relevance to this book is the work of Philips (1972a, 1972b, 1983), which makes an important contribution to the scholarship in this field. Philips' research addresses the issue of learning problems in the classroom. One result of her research is a partial explanation for the discrepancies in national test scores, in which the Warm Springs Reservation students scored consistently lower than their Euro-American classmates (Erickson & Mohatt 1982:140; Philips 1983:13). The culmination of her study revealed that the Warm Springs Indian students had culturally defined modes of communication and participation that had a tremendous influence on their classroom behavior (Philips 1983:19). It is this discovery of a different participation style which makes Native American education such a fertile field for research.

This area in particular, ancestral language learning in light of the participation and learning preferences, is what I address in this research. I want to consider these questions concerning the learning of Haida: Do the Haida students exhibit differences with Euro-Canadians in their participation styles? If so, how do their Haida learning and participation styles affect ancestral language learning?

Significant to Philips' observation is the idea that the Warm Springs Indian students' home life explains their differences and difficulties in the classroom. She remarks that the question "Why don't Indian kids talk more in class?" is, in a sense, a very simple one (1972a:372) and suggests that speech conditions in the community are different than they are in the classroom. Thus, a blend of learning styles and social conditions for speech combine to affect the students' interaction patterns in the classroom (392).

In her research, Philips (1972a:371; 1983:39) noted that the socialization process on the reservation differs from that of the Euro-Americans off the reservation. The Warm Springs Indian students had had six years of socialization practices that quickly came into conflict with those at school. Philips observed differences immediately upon the child's first year at the school. The initial differences concerned the expected behaviors to which the Warm Springs children had to adjust. It is worthwhile to cite at length the first interests of the teacher, as Philips notes:

> When the children first enter school the most immediate concern of the teachers is to teach them the basic rules for classroom behavior upon which the maintenance of continuous and ordered activity depends. One of the most important of these is the distinction and implicit assumption that the teacher controls all of the activity taking place in the classroom and the students accept and are obedient to her authority. She determines the sociospatial arrangements of all interactions; she decrees when and where movement takes place within the classroom. And most important for our present concern of communication, she determines who will talk and when they will talk. (Philips 1972a:375)

These basic rules and expectations of the teachers are ultimately and immediately a source of conflict for the Warms Springs Indian students and Philips comments that the differences in learning these basic rules are "immediately apparent" (1972a:376). The fact that it is necessary for teachers to instill the rules and set themselves up as the seat of authority and attention contrasts with the Warm Springs Indian students' social patterns at home. It is unusual for one person to be the center of such control in a gathering with as many people as one finds in the classroom. Though there are community functions that focus attention on speakers, these are normally not formal settings and the children could attend to the gatherings or interact with the other children present as they pleased.

Concerning the classroom rules, Philips notes that Native American first graders are "consistently slower" in obeying the teacher. This may in fact be a result of their not having such a central authority figure demanding attention and compliance at home. She mentions that the Native American children also speak up without raising their hands and waiting to be called upon, they wander throughout the class in the midst of a lesson, and they fail to conform to classroom procedure throughout their first year. The Warm Springs Reservation social life at home does not require formality for speech, such as raising hands; neither do Euro-American family settings, but it seems to be easier for Euro-Americans to adjust to this requirement than for the Warm Springs Indian students. As far as wandering around the classroom, the socialization pattern at home, in the family, and in community gatherings allows children individual autonomy and the classroom restrictions conflict with the freedom that they have previously enjoyed. Their inability to conform to the classroom setting is a measure of the length of time it takes to adjust to the new social system, i.e., it takes almost all year, and Philips notes the frustration of the teachers on this point.

Philips also observes that the Warm Springs children are more interested in what other students are doing than what the teacher is doing. Again, this may simply reflect the traditional process of socialization in which peers are the ones who normally share and are the center of attention. Attending to demands of a stranger, one who does not have the cultural authority to make such demands due to a lack of kinship or even a recognizable relationship, is extremely foreign to the Warm Springs Indian student. As a result, the students are more interested in those with whom they are familiar.

Philips notes other significant differences, one of which includes the extent to which the students bid for the teacher's attention, or openly seek the teacher's consideration during lessons through dialogue or other means. The Euro-American students excel at the competitive nature of securing the right to speak, or getting the teacher's attention, which contrasts with the Warm Spring children's lack of such attempts. The competitive practice of displaying knowledge, to win the teacher's approval, is not evident among the Warm Springs Indian students (1983:109). This factor causes great consternation in teachers when they try to educate Native American children according to the competitive model and meet only silence as a result of the lack of students' interest in displaying their knowledge. The Warm Springs Indian students are more prone to bid for the attention of their fellow students, and at times seemingly act in complete discord with the teacher's directions.

The difference between Native American and Euro-American student participation becomes noticeable during the classroom lessons and the teachers' "use of participant structures" (Philips 1972a:377). Philips considers four different types of structures that she has observed, noting that in the first type,

> the teacher interacts with all the students...She may address all...or a single student in the presence of the other students. They may respond as a group, or chorus in unison, or individually in the presence of peers. And finally, the verbal participation may be either involuntary, as when the teacher asks a particular student to answer, whether his hand is raised or not...the teacher...determines whether she talks to one or all, receives responses individually or in chorus, and voluntarily or without choice. (1972b:377)

Interaction with a large group may not be so problematic for the Warm Springs students, nor so unusual, but there are things that would make such settings foreign, like being required to answer when called upon. A normal Native American educational setting would allow voluntary participation at the discretion of the student, and the speaker would normally observe such constraints without reserve. A song might normally be sung by all the children, but it would be in unison, not normally by one child chosen and called upon by the speaker. The important factor to note is that the teacher is always in control of the classroom's speaking environment and is the one who decides who says anything and when they say it.

The second type of participant structure restricts the teacher's addressees. With a group activity, the teacher may focus on that group while the other students are doing individual desk work. The students' verbal participation in this context is mandatory rather than voluntary (Philips 1972a:377). This involuntarily required speech conflicts with the autonomy normally given to children in the home setting. The result is usually met with silence, or with barely audible utterances. This second structure's function is "to provide the teacher with the opportunity to assess the knowledge acquired by each individual student" (Philips 1983:80). The Warms Springs students suffer greatly from this assessment. Due to their lack of participation, the assessments are not very favorable, because the basis for evaluation includes aspects of participation that are in conflict with their native socialization patterns.

A third type of structure is the one-on-one interaction of the teacher and the student. This type of interaction happens during desk work, usually on a first-come, first-served basis initiated either by hand raising or approaching the teacher's desk (Philips: 1983:81). The one-on-one or face-to-face interaction is generally more acceptable and reflects the community interaction pattern for most Native Americans. For this reason, one-on-one is perhaps the most acceptable format for the Warm Springs Indian students as they are more prone to approach the teacher in private without having to be the center of attention with everyone present focused on their participation (Philips 1972b:172). For many Native American students, being able to approach the teacher in private consultation ranks high on their participation preference scale (Philips 1972b:379).

The final participant structure is what Philips suggests is participation through desk work in which the focus is upon reading written materials. The visual channel (i.e., reading) has priority over the auditory channel (i.e., listening). The stimulation comes from the written material that is being read silently. This particular structure has its benefits and its drawbacks. What is good about it, from the teacher's perspective, is that it promotes individual development, and, at the same time, provides a breather for the teacher. He or she can mentally prepare for the next activity as well as monitor the reading. What is problematic is that the children, not necessarily only the Warm Springs students, may not want to read and thus can easily be distracted from the activity.

The advantages and disadvantages of each participant structure manifest themselves during the lesson as the teachers' expectation for student involvement meets resistance from the Warm Springs students; the typical response is usually inaudible utterances, or silence. Both reactions are problematic, but especially silence. Literature written about the silence of the Native American student in the class is helpful (see Chiang 1993; Plank 1994; Swisher & Deyhle 1989), revealing that the teachers' expectations of participation usually conflict with the patterns of participation the students have been socialized into and that the students' transition in the classroom is not yet complete (Wauters, Bruce, Black & Hoover 1989:54). This conflict is probably most evident when the teacher queries the students for information or participation and then singles out a Native American student, who most likely did not volunteer any answers or did not raise his or her hand. The teacher, expecting an answer, hears only silence. For the teacher, this limits his or her assessment to thinking the child does not know the answer, or is not living up to his or her potential. Or the teacher, knowing that the child knows the answer, thinks he or she is just being non-cooperative.

To address the deeper, cultural reasons for the lack of response to the teacher's queries, it is important to know why the Native American children do not voluntarily compete in the classroom or respond immediately to the teacher's demands for answers to her queries. In most Native American Indian societies, making yourself look smarter than others is not culturally acceptable (Dumont 1972:353). In the classroom, when a Native American student is singled out, the response is usually silence rather than the display of knowledge or skills the teacher wants, which frustrates the teacher (Crago 1992:497; Dumont: 1972:345; Erickson & Mohatt 1981). In such a setting it is not acceptable when an individual displays knowledge that would make others look bad because they do not know the answer. Many times the student prefers not to answer, thereby keeping face with the other Native students, but losing face with the teacher. The point is that these typical expectations and participation structures are not conducive for Native American participation and learning in the classroom. This fact has tremendous relevance concerning the process of the Haidas' learning their ancestral language and will be addressed again in the discussion section.

A very poignant example from my observations in Masset also confirmed such reluctance and provided amazing conformity to many other observations that Philips and others have recorded. During one period of the combined sixth and seventh grade Haida lesson, I observed a very loud, boisterous, and confident Haida girl, Tracy (all names referring to any instructors, teachers, or students are pseudonyms as part of the agreement made with the instructors). She was not participating in the lesson per se, but was nonetheless active in talking with her friends and ignoring the Haida instructors. One of the instructors rebuked her for her loudness and reprimanded her lack of attention to the lesson. I followed the class to their next lesson, Language Arts, and the required assignment for that day was an oral report or, in any case of lack of preparation, reading in front of the class. When it came time for Tracy's presentation, her demeanor and presence had changed dramatically. She immediately exuded reluctance, timidity, and a lack of confidence and when she started to read, it was barely above a whisper. As she read, I had to strain to hear her, but even then, only a few words were clear enough to be distinguishable. The teacher admonished her to speak louder, but her volume did not noticeably increase. Tracy's reluctance and demeanor exemplified most Native American students' reaction to being singled out and put on the spot.

The current research here on the Haida provides an analysis that supports work that Philips has done, as well as others, including Dumont's (1972) examination of the Sioux and Cherokee. He suggests that participation and silence were tremendously misunderstood by the teachers (1972:344), and most notably that the current education system would only be detrimental to any educational or economic achievement because the approach does nothing but alienate the students, not only from American culture, but from their own culture as well (1972:368). John (1972) agrees with Dumont in suggesting that the teaching methodology and teacher's expectation serve only to increase the lack of participation and exacerbate what she termed "miseducation" (John 1972:331). I, therefore, address the Haida instructors' methodology as well as the Haida student styles of participation in order to ultimately enhance both instructor and student benefit from the Haida lessons.

In other related research, paralleling Philips' notion of distinct participation styles, Arlene Stairs' (1993) research with the North Baffin Inuit suggests that in order to address the learning style difference, it is necessary to provide both a cultural base and brokerage for the students. The cultural base includes "cultural values concerning ways of using language, of interacting, and of knowing" (1993:86). Stairs deems "brokerage" as a blending of traditional and formal learning into a new role of a "native educator." Her attention to the cultural blending of learning with practices in the classroom fosters hope for greater Native American student participation success in the formal educational process (Stairs 1993:98).

In his research, including that among the Okanagan/Nicola, More (1989) agrees with Philips' notions of different learning styles and Stairs' notion of brokerage, and recognizes that the traditional learning setting, the environment (1989:21), differs from the new formal approach setting. He suggests that an integration of the two settings would be beneficial for the educational progress of the Native American student (1989:26).

Wauters, Bruce, Black, & Hocker's (1989) work with Alaskan Natives confirms their preference for a collaborative learning approach and small group tasks. In contrast to the non-Alaskan students, the authors note, "Although both groups are well within the norm for preference for learning with peers, Native students are significantly more peer-oriented than nonNatives." They suggest "small group work such as discussion circles and collaborative writing assignments can be encouraged. Peer tutoring might be a helpful strategy as well" (1989:60). Their conclusion addresses the problem of attrition for Native Americans in education and they propose, "matching instructional techniques to learning styles is one positive step in this direction" (Wauters, Bruce, Black, & Hocker 1989:61).

Overall, Philips' conclusion concerning basic classroom behavior is that the Warms Springs children "were less willing to accept the teacher as director and controller of all classroom activity" (1972a:377). This rejection of authority manifested in their behavior, though appropriate and acceptable at home and in their community, is extremely unwelcome in the classroom. The Warm Springs Indian student behavior creates problems and results in evaluations that are not necessarily true, such as the children not wanting to learn, or, even worse, their being incapable of learning. But Philips notes the Warm Springs Indian students are reluctant to speak in the classroom as a result of having a different pattern of socialization that directly affected their performance and participation in the classroom. Teachers in North America have benefited from her research and from the later research it inspired, including: Arthur More's review of learning styles for researchers and teachers (1989); Stairs' cultural brokerage approach to teaching Native Americans (1993); Karen Swisher's review of cooperative learning and education literature of American Indian/Alaskan Natives and her suggestions for pedagogical implementations in mixed (native and nonnative) classrooms (1990); and Frederick Erickson and Gerald Mohatt's work in which they discuss similarities and differences of cultural organization of social relationships, focusing on the differences and effects of the teachers' different cultural background and the manner in which each teacher exercised authority in their classrooms (1986). These four are representative of the vast field Philips directly or indirectly influenced as a result of her research.

Summary

Philips' work provided a great impetus for studies that addressed learning style differences. She made it very clear that there were various cultural influences that account for participation differences in the classroom. Later research confirmed her findings and though none actually applied her findings specifically to language learning, I springboard from her results, and the research that followed, to assess the impact of these style differences on Haida students learning their ancestral language as a second language.

Philips' summary concerning the Warm Springs Indians is most important to this research. Addressing the issue of teaching methodology, she notes:

> Surprisingly little attention has been given to the teaching
> methods used in teaching ethnic minority students in this
> country, particularly when the notion of culturally relevant
> curriculum materials has been around as long as it has. It is as if
> we have been able to recognize that there are cultural differences
> in what people learn, but not in how they learn. (1982:133)

My purpose, therefore, is to assume that Haidas participate differently than their non-Haida classmates and that that such participatory differences have a significant impact on their learning Haida as a second language in a classroom setting.

In summary, I am providing a list of Native American students' participatory preferences pooled from the literature. It is not an exhaustive list that includes items every Native American student exhibits, but represents important differences that influence their behavior in the classroom. My interest is to compare and contrast the results of similar research with my Haida data. Native American students have a tendency to:

1. Participate at their own discretion, i.e:, they are prone to engage or assert themselves when they want to (Philips 1972a:378; Wolcott 1974:413). The negative side of this is that they will not participate when they do not want to (Cleary & Peacock 1998; Whyte 1986:3).

2. Enjoy tasks that are group oriented (Le Brasseur & Freark 1982:9). They commit themselves to greater interaction when they are in small peer groups (Wolcott 1974:414). As a result, they benefit more from a collaborative learning approach (Plank 1994:3; Sawyer 1990).

3. Favor one-on-one interaction with the teacher for clarification or for permission (Browne 1990:30). Most often, the strategy employed for this clarification is a face-to-face query in which the student has the sole attention of the teacher for permission, e.g., going to the restroom (Philips 1972a:379).

4. Prefer to participate out loud when comfortable enough with the subject (Kaulback 1984:32-3). They must sense that they can competently perform or answer the teacher before they will venture to do so (Philips 1983:113).

5. Learn from repeated and silent observation (Pepper & Henry 1987:57). They listen quietly to stories, songs (Macias 1989:48), or watch how to solve math problems, draw an eagle, or tie knots until they are ready to try to do the task themselves (Hirst & Slavik 1990; Stairs 1993:87).

6. Be spatially and holistically (or gestalt) oriented rather than linearly and analytically oriented (Pepper & Henry 1987:58). Ross suggests that many Native Americans are right-brain dominant (1982:2) and prefer location in space rather than location in time, they make pictorial & pattern sense rather than abstractions, and they look for visual similarities rather than conceptual similarities (Diessner & Walker 1986).

7. Prefer holistic approaches to learning piecemeal (Wilgosh & Mulcahy 1993:132). The western approach is systematic and sequentially organized (for example concerning English grammatical instruction, see Toohey & Allen 1985:656), but many times fails to provide the scope of what the teacher will teach, i.e., the whole picture, which native students prefer seeing (Friesen, Archibald & Jack, 1992:19; Rhodes 1988:22; Sawyer, 1990).

8. Be interested in what other students are doing rather than what the teacher is doing (Yamuchi & Tharp 1995:355). In their transition to the classroom, first grade Native American students take longer to accept

the teacher as the sole authority of the classroom and as a result, prefer to pay attention to or get the attention of other students (Philips 1983:128).

9. Take their time (more than their non-Native American classmates) to respond to teacher queries (Yamuchi & Tharp 1995:354). If the teacher has the patience to wait for an answer, the wait time is longer for the Native American students than their other classmates (Erickson & Mohatt 1982/88:144).

10. Remain silent when being reproached. In Native American tribes, as with most people, being corrected is an embarrassing situation (Philips 1983:107). The difference is the avoidance of eye contact and lack of vocal responses during such experiences (Plank 1994:10).

11. Spurn displaying knowledge that others may not have (Tafoya 1989:31). The western competitive mode of education often requires vocal responses to satisfy the teacher's request for knowledge displays (Swisher & Deyhle 1989). This command performance, or showing off, is not acceptable because it may make others look bad, or the student answering look too smart, both of which are culturally inappropriate (Philips 1972b; Leavitt, 1995; Wolcott 1974:414).

12. In light of 11, students prefer not being "spotlighted" i.e., being singled out for mandatory or involuntary participation (Philips 1972a:382 & 1983:119; Yamuchi & Tharp 1995:354). Most often spotlighting brings about a long silence before a response, an incorrect response, or no response (Shutiva 1991:37).

13. Participate more in learning that is not competitively structured (Browne 1990:30). The students are much more apt to put forth effort when they can interact with their peers (LeBrasseur & Freark 1982:9: Sawyer 1990; Shutiva 1991:37).

14. Wander around the class without permission (Philips 1972a:376). This issue, in reference to 8, reveals the Native American students' tendency

to disregard the social constraints the teacher has imposed upon the classroom (Philips 1972a:391).

In this book, I am particularly interested in Native American student tendencies: 1. to participate at their own discretion; 2. to enjoy tasks that are group oriented, 4. to prefer to participate out loud when comfortable enough with the subject; and 11. to spurn displaying knowledge that others may not have. These characteristics are significant to my interest in considering how each item affects both participation and language learning, and I will address them in depth as I analyze the Haida lessons in chapter five. I shall also address the subsequent points in more detail in my analysis of the Haida lessons.

Chapter 2
Haida Historical Background

General history

Haida Gwaii, which literally means the islands of the Haidas, is a northwesterly Canadian archipelago chain in the Pacific Ocean. The setting of this study is in two different locations: Skidegate and Masset, both on Haida Gwaii, British Columbia, but emphasis is given to Skidegate for the data I analyze. Haida history dates back to "mythtime" preserved in the oral tradition of creation stories, songs, ceremonies, history and mythology of the tribe. The curator of the National Museum of Canada suggests that the Haida presence on Haida Gwaii spans 9,000 years (Johnson 1987:115). An exodus of some Haida to Alaska within the last 400 years (Cogo & Cogo 1983:33), has the Kaigani Haida living state side.

In 1774 contact with Euro-Americans began (Beals 1989:3). The contact was sparse at first, escalating to the typical trade contact, and followed by the newly formed Canadian governmental surveyors as the land was deemed "crown land". Finally, missionary contact began in approximately 1876 (Collison 1981:57). In the midst of the escalating contact, a smallpox epidemic, which began in the mid 1860s and lasted until the turn of the century, wiped out 90-94% of the Haida population (Beals 1989:65; Blackman 1982:44-45; Van Der Brink 1974:44, 82-83). Contact with the missionaries, as well as the newly established provincial and federal government, began an era of colonialism that initiated attempts to eradicate Haida culture and language in a systematic effort to assimilate the Haidas (and all Native American peoples) into the newly developing Canadian culture (Boelscher 1989:193; Lilliard 1989:27; Van Der Brink 27

Recently the islands have officially secured the traditional name, Haida Gwaii, though most maps still designate the area as the Queen Charlotte Islands.

Language background.

Since the last quarter of the nineteenth century, Haida has received a considerable degree of attention. Scholarly investigations of Haida, from geological surveyors to missionaries to linguists, have produced a vast body of literature analyzing everything from Haida's phonemic inventory to its grammatical structure.

George Dawson and Fraser Tolmie, geological surveyors, compiled one of the earliest lists of Haida vocabulary which they published in 1884 entitled *Comparative vocabularies of the Indian tribes of British Columbia, with a map illustrating distribution.*

Charles Harrison's missionary efforts included publications concerning Haida grammar (1895). He wrote that the

principal object in writing this grammar is to afford assistance to

my successors in mission work amongst the Haidas, and those

who may desire to gain a knowledge of the language in order to

benefit these Indians both temporally and spiritually. (1895:126)

In keeping with his "principal object," Harrison also published Haida translations of parts of the Bible (mostly from the New Testament), such as the *The Gospel according to St. John* (1899) and *The Acts of the Apostles in Haida* (1898).

At the turn of the century, John Swanton, under the tutelage of Franz Boas, began an ethnographic study of the Haida (1905a) and published a comprehensive body of work. His work included a grammar of Haida (1911) as well as translated stories and songs from both the Masset (1908) and Skidegate (1905b) dialects.

Swanton's collections and publications contain by far the most information, history, ethnology, songs, and myths.

Since Swanton, there have been a number of substantial linguistic works concerning Haida. The Alaska Native Language Center published a Haida dictionary in the Kaigani dialect (Lawrence and Leer 1977). The dictionary was a result of a collective need of the Haida community in Alaska. Haida instructors and individuals studying Haida had

> been asking for some kind of dictionary to help them get started, so
> as a first effort at a unified Haida dictionary, we present here a
> preliminary list of many common words and a few uncommon
> ones for the benefit of the beginning learner. (1977:5)

To date, there have also been four dissertations examining different linguistic aspects of Haida. Daniel Anker reviews Haida kinship terminology (1975) in his dissertation. Limiting his database to written works from 1900-1974, Anker compiled, compared, and analyzed kinship lexical morphology beginning with Swanton's earliest published research.

Robert Levine's dissertation (1977) concerns the Skidegate dialect. Levine worked primarily with four speakers. He discusses phonology, nominals, predicates, and particles, as well as analyzing Skidegate narratives. Levine also discusses Haida in its areal context and provides an index of affixes and particles.

John James Enrico's dissertation examines the Masset dialect's phonology (1980). Part of his interest is comparative in nature, as he states that "part of the work in Masset has been the reworking and analysis of all of Swanton's large and extremely valuable collection of Masset material" (p. XIV). He then explains that his research "was done with one goal being its possible use by the Masset people" (XIV).

Elizabeth Edwards (1982), author of the most recent study, analyzed *The Importance of Pragmatic Factors in Haida Syntax*. Using a functional approach, she argued that any analysis using only grammatical concepts fails to account for

Haida constituent order. Pragmatic factors such as topic and information focus, Edwards argues, prove more effective in determining Haida constituent order than purely syntactic or grammatical factors.

Numerous articles have also been written on Haida grammar, including Carol M. Eastman's "Word order in Haida" (1979a); Herman Karl Haeberlin's "Notes on the composition of the verbal complex in Haida" (1923); Joseph F. Kess' "Pronominal systems in Haida" (1974); and Robert J. Welsch's "Haida pronouns-Hydaburg dialect" (1975), just to name a few.

Originally classified as Na-Dene, the subject of Haida's classification is still controversial. Sapir, based on what he learned from Swanton and Boas, assumed Haida, Tlingit, and Athabaskan had "important morphological, and to a lesser extent lexical, resemblances" (1915:534). He explained the name of the classification as compound of *Dene* meaning 'people' in the Athabaskan languages and the element *na,* an old stem which also meant 'people' in Tlingit and 'house' in Haida. "The compound term 'Na-Dene' thus designates by means of native stems the speakers of the three languages concerned," he explained, adding "besides continuing the use of the old term 'Dene' for the Athabaskan branch of the stock" (Sapir 1915:558).

Recent research and re-evaluation has generated a controversy with some researchers wanting Haida to be reclassified as an isolate (see Levine 1979; Campbell 1990). Levine has suggested that Sapir relied too heavily on Navajo data for comparisons and that he had assumed relatedness to Tlingit and Athabaskan based on methodological flaws (Levine 1979:171). He suggested that if there is proof that Haida is Na-Dene, it has not been submitted. Manaster Ramer, on the other hand, countered that it is too early to reject Sapir's classification and that it may be a matter of time before the evidence will justify Sapir (Ramer 1996:210).

There are thus two camps regarding this issue: those who see Haida as Na-Dene (Sapir 1915; Hymes 1956) and those see it as an isolate (Levine 1979; Campbell 1990).

According to his analysis, Swanton (1908:274) suggested that the Haida phonemic inventory had a total of 46 different phonemes, 18 of which were vowels. Sapir, "supplementing Dr. Swanton's brief statement" after only a few hours with Peter R. Kelly, a Skidegate Haida man, suggested that Haida had 47 consonants (Sapir 1923:145). In his analysis of the vowel system, Sapir suggested that there were "only three organically distinct vowels" (1923:154) and two diphthongs (1923:156). Swanton's phonemic inventory sketch, rather than Sapir's, ultimately became the model for subsequent research.

Current Haida research, which also addresses the Haida phonemic inventory, includes Enrico's efforts to gather data for a new Haida dictionary. Enrico suggests that the Skidegate dialect "preserves some of the consonants lost in the northern dialects...Similarly, the Masset dialect preserves certain consonants or skeletal slots that have been lost in the Alaskan dialect" (Enrico 1994:3). He suggests that the Skidegate dialect is the most conservative and states that this dialect will be first in the dictionary because it provides insights regarding the lost consonant forms of the northern dialect. He explains that the current simplified Haida orthography results from consonant loss and a change from a tone system in Canada (Haida Gwaii) to a pitch accent system in Alaska (Hydaburg and Ketchikan) (Enrico 1994:3).

Concerning its morphosyntactic features, Haida has a subject-object-verb (SOV) structure, or, depending on the scholar, an object-subject-verb (OSV) structure. Swanton suggests that the verb "almost always stands at the end of the sentence or clause" (1911:267). Swanton also suggested that the word order is SOV for nominal constituents and OSV for pronominal constituents. The first example from his collection seems to contradict his observation:

K!iūsta	*gu*	*Ildī'nī*	*na'gan.*
End of trail(Town)	at	Ildī'nī	lived.
O		S	V

Ildī'nī lived at Kiusta. (Swanton 1905b:15)

The next example also seems to contradict his observation, but upon closer inspection, if the independent pronoun is considered nominal, it conforms to the SOV structure.

> *La'hoa L!*   *sūga*   *sqā'djigAn*
> He   them   among   was a brave man
> S   O   V
> He was a brave man among them. (Swanton 1911:277)

Edwards (1983) notes the confusion which results from traditional analysis of subject and object with regards to Haida word order and suggests that contextual factors influence understanding Haida utterances. She provides the following example for consideration,

> *Fred taanaay tiigaan*
> Fred bear   killed
> a. *Fred* killed the bear.
> b. The bear killed Fred. (1983:150)

Edwards then explains that these two sentences (sentences b and d do not have any bearing on our discussion here, thus, I included only a and c) could be the answer to the question, "who killed the bear kill?" as well as the question "who did the bear kill?" since both questions are represented by the same utterance in Haida,

> *gissduu tanaay tiiaayan*
> who   bear   killed
> a. Who killed the bear?
> b. Who did the bear kill? (1983:151).

Thus, Edwards concludes that,

> While discussions of constituent order in Haida in terms of the
> grammatical categories Subject and Object are inclusive, the
> identification of the sentence-initial constituent as the
> information focus allows us to explain the apparent

contradictions in word order proposed by Swanton. (Edwards 1983:156)

In another analysis, Eastman (1979a) observes it has been accepted that Haida has an OSV word order and provides her first example as evidence,

(1) *chiin hl taagaang*

    fish   I   eat

    O   S   V

    I eat fish. (1979a:141)

Eastman also confirms Swanton's observation (1911: 267) that when nouns and pronouns are both used as subjects and objects, the pronouns usually stand nearest to the verb. She provides examples, the first of which demonstrates adherence to Swanton's rule (the example number reflects her numbering),

(2) *xagyaa l daawaang*

    dog   they   have + present

    O   S   V

    They have a dog. (1979a:142)

Thus, her analysis seems to confirm an OSV word order.

Edwards provides other examples which challenge that classification. These two examples provided here represent her evidence for an SOV word order (the example numbers reflect her own numbering),

(15) *yaalaay skaangway iisdang*

    the raven   the stick   take + present

    S   O   V

    The raven is taking the stick.

(19) *nang iihlingas kiiksgaay taa'aasaan*

    the man   the cake   eat + directional + future

    S   O   V

    The man will go eat the cake. (Edwards 1979a:144)

Eastman asserts "that Haida is a topic-prominent language in which a Sentence is analyzed as (Topic) + Comment" (1979a:147). She concludes that "Haida as a topic-prominent language may best be analyzed as having no one basic order in terms of the order of meaningful elements in sentences, although both an SOV and OSV order are common" (1979a:148).

Levine, challenging the classification through closer structural analysis, suggests that "the proper generalization is that the order of constituents, in sentences containing person markers rather than nouns, is XSOV in most cases" but he goes on to explain that "X includes indirect objects, locational, temporal and adverbial material, embedded clauses and so on" (1979:161). Though the argument continues, the final analysis is clearly that Haida is verb final in structure, as Campbell notes (1990:1032).

Haida, like many other Native American languages, is currently at a critical stage of possible language death. There are at present few fluent speakers left in Skidegate and Masset. Only 15-20% of the elders (Report of the Assembly of First Nations language and literacy secretariat, 1992:64,73) are fluent. Of these speakers, nearly 95% are over 55 and are female. There are no monolingual Haida speakers left.

Finally, the Haida instructors' orthography, represented in the transcripts, results from a modified orthography found in the *Haida Dictionary* (Lawrence & Leer 1977) and in consultation with Enrico and his research (1980; 1994). Concerning the Haida transcription, Enrico and Stuart's (1996:x-xii) orthographic notes are helpful in realizing pronunciation. I have modified their chart (found in the LIST OF SYMBOLS, p. vii) by adding descriptions and a modified IPA equivalent in brackets [] after each description.

Educational background

As with many societies, education was originally informal and lifelong. The elders passed on knowledge from one generation to the next. This knowledge included the language, as well as the tribe's history, traditions, songs, and survival skills. The role of the learner was that of an observer/apprentice. Until the student had the confidence to participate, his or her role was mainly observational; after which the student would become a participant or a participant observer (Beck, Walters, & Francisco 1992:56).

Formal education began on Haida Gwaii during the last decades of the 1800s. The implementation of formal education was gradual, often resulting in removal of children from their parents then bringing them to a residential school for Native American children (Collison 1993:36). Quite often, they were not only taken away from family and friends, but they were taken to a foreign location, usually hundreds or even thousands of miles from home (Bell 1993:8).

When the newly formed Canadian dominion government intervened in the process, governmental restrictions and ceremonial bans began in the latter part of the 1870s (Van Der Brink 1989:72). Then, with the advent of residential schools, the government ruthlessly implemented methodical cultural reprogramming that targeted every aspect of Native American culture. The last Canadian residential school closed in the late 1960s.

This education began with the stated goal of civilizing the Haida. As the Twentieth Century began, the efforts to civilize the students invariably included the elimination of every aspect of life that the children had known. They had to endure a process of resocialization which included a harsh transition from an informal mode of learning to a formal mode (More 1989:21; Suino 1988). The students had to speak English and only English, or, once again, swift punishment resulted (see Achneepineskum 1993:2; Bell 1993:10). Life, for the Haidas, would never be the same (Stearns: 1984:6).

During the last two decades, there has been tremendous political recognition of Native American issues. The most prominent are land, mineral, fishing and hunting rights (Cahill 1993:98; Johnson 1987:116; Stearns 1981:12) and most important to this paper, education. In 1972, there was official governmental acknowledgment of the need to preserve the culture and history of the Native American peoples of Canada (Fourth report of the standing committee on aboriginal affairs, 1990:14). In particular, educational efforts and reforms included providing relevant history, art, science, and language from the Native American perspective for each geographical area. This initiated efforts at the grassroots level to include teaching the Native American languages in school. Near the end of the 1980's, the Haida Gwaii school district implemented efforts at maintaining the Haida language at school. The program was active through the 1990's, though the language instruction provided is currently available only through the elementary grades.

Current Haida social patterns in the home

Commenting on the current patterns of socialization on Haida Gwaii, Stearns, in her book *Haida culture in custody: The Masset Band,* suggested that the adaptations she observed were resulting in tremendous cultural loss (1981:6). What she noted was a process of assimilation that endangered forms of Haida expression (Stearns 1981:292). But even with the cultural losses, patterns of socialization remain distinct from those found in mainstream Canada.

Childhood for the Haida reserve children consists of growing up in a household marked by noticeable similarities to Philips' observations about the rearing of Warm Springs Indian children. Some of the similarities include,

1. Parents are not the only ones responsibly caring for the children. Older siblings and other relatives, including parental siblings, aunts, uncles, and grandparents often share child-rearing responsibilities (Blackman 1982:81).

2. Children interact with and adhere to more figures of authority than is the case with non-Indian children (Stearns 1981:137). As the children interact with elder siblings as well as cousins (mother's sister's children), aunts (mother's sisters), uncles (mother's brothers), and grandparents (mother's parents), they learn to respect their authority (Blackman 1982:95).

3. Most of the people involved in the child-rearing process are kin, aside from siblings, the list includes cousins, aunts, uncles, and grandparents (Blackman 1982:83).

4. The children are rarely watched by baby-sitters outside of the family. With the extensive kinship system guiding the interaction, it is infrequent for a baby-sitter to be needed outside the family (Stearns 1981:139).

5. Most of the child's playmates before entering school are siblings, other family, or other Haidas living on the reserve (field notes 1994). Since the reserve provides a very isolated community setting most often the interaction with others is kinship based and most certainly, exclusively Haida until they enter school.

6. Haida children are accustomed to self-determination with little or no disciplinary actions. The current form of disciplinary action is mainly "talking to them" with the idea that whatever the problem is simply requires a verbal straightening out (Stearns 1981:76).

7. Haida children often attend community events with parents no matter how late the event ends (field notes 1993).

8. The Haidas experience a distribution of leadership in community events as opposed to a Master of Ceremonies approach with one leader.

9. Participation in community events is usually open ended, i.e., anyone who wants to participate can when he or she wants. The gatherings at the local band office (for both Masset and Skidegate) are usually informal and allow participation on the part of anyone attending the meetings (field notes 1993-4).

10. The community has a three-step approach to learning simple skills, such as light cooking and fishing: (1) from observation,

(2) from supervised participation, and (3) from private self-initiating trials (Blackman 1982).

Some of the social interaction patterns that vary from Philips' observations ultimately reflect greater encroachment of Canadian and American pop culture. Specifically, the entertainment media now has a tremendous impact on the children before they enter school. They are most likely to have had exposure to television (controlled by older siblings and parents) including *Sesame Street*, *Arthur*, *Pokémon*, and other such programs. Movies also are common place since most households have television and video cassette recorders. Exposure to contemporary music (especially older siblings' preferences) also influences children's environment prior to their formal education.

Even with the pop culture's encroachment on the current situation, the cultural similarities shared by the Haida students account for a background that is markedly different from their non-Haida Euro-Canadian classmates. These differences ultimately affect their learning and participation in the classroom.

Current school conditions on Haida Gwaii

The current school conditions on Haida Gwaii reveal interesting differences between the two main villages. Masset has two elementary schools and a high school. The newer Chief Matthews Elementary School, which has Kindergarten to third grade students, is the only school located on the Massett reserve (anything referring to the reserve or the Band Council has "Massett" with the last letter doubled). The other schools, Tahaygen Elementary School and George M. Dawson Secondary School, are approximately two miles away in New Masset (spelled with one "t").

The Haida language program is optional in Masset. Students leave their regular classroom and go to the Haida language room to learn Haida.

The ratio of Haida teachers and instructors to mainstream teachers and instructors is about 1 to 10 in Masset and 1 to 5 in Skidegate (at the elementary school). In both Masset and Skidegate, the language program is only for Kindergarten through seventh grade. A choice between Haida or French is available in Masset, but French is an "academic preference" of the parents because French meets most university foreign language requirements. Only recently have British Columbia universities recognized and allowed First Nations languages to meet a "foreign" language requirement. Despite this recent policy change, many parents continue to endorse an English only approach to their children's education.

Skidegate

Skidegate originally had only one elementary school and one high school in a combined facility. The two schools divided into separate schools beginning with the 1999 school year: The Sk'aadgaa Naay Elementary School and Queen Charlotte Secondary School. There are thirteen teachers and two Haida instructors at Sk'aadgaa Naay Elementary School. The Haida instructors are not employed as teachers, but as instructors through the Skidegate Band Council. Prior to the division, the combined school population had an average of approximately 400 students since September of 1990.

The Haida language instructors do not have their own room. Instead they go to the different regular classrooms and provide Haida lessons while the mainstream teacher takes a break and leaves the room, or stays behind and prepares material for the class after the Haida class, or in some cases participates in the Haida lesson. For Skidegate students, participation in the Haida language program is not optional.

Chapter 3
Methodology

Ethnography

The compounded Greek terms "ethnos", meaning 'nation', or literally peoples, and "graphein", meaning 'to write', combine to form the anthropological term "ethnography" 'Ethnology', its precursor, has the same prefix but with 'logos', meaning word, as a second element. Ethnological publications began near the turn of the nineteenth century specifically for the purpose of studying distinct cultures. The Bureau of Ethnology, as part of the Smithsonian Institution, exemplifies this genre with its first publication in 1871. Swanton's *Contributions to the Ethnology of the Haida, #40* (1911) also conforms to this early stage of ethnology. The fourfold purpose of ethnology is to describe, explain, compare and interpret cultures both synchronically and historically.

Ethnography limited its focus to living peoples in order to investigate: 1. how they live, 2. what they do, 3. what they believe, 4. how they interact, and 5. what objects they use. The term then began to expand its boundaries in terms of subjects of study, and subsequently, the American classroom began to be a target of ethnography (Erickson & Mohatt 1982/88; Spindler & Spindler 1982/88; Wilcox 1982/88). It is in this tradition that I base the structure of this book. I am not suggesting this is an ethnography of the Haida classroom, rather, I hope to glean from these disciplines in order to provide a foundation for exploring and establishing groundwork for such ethnographic research.

I also glean insight from several discourse analysis traditions (Duranti 1985:193; Ochs 1979:43; Sacks, Schegloff and Jefferson 1974) as well and, therefore, fuse the analysis of language interaction into my classroom analysis.

The beginning of my involvement

As a child, I can remember vividly visiting *nani* and *tsini* (Haida terms which do not discriminate paternal and maternal ascendants, see Stearns [1981:219]), my grandparents, and upon arriving at their house, all my aunts and uncles began speaking Haida. It was a very curious situation since I did not speak Haida and neither did any of my siblings or my cousins. In 1974, after the death of both grandparents, I noticed that my aunts and uncles were not speaking Haida anymore when they gathered.

I never thought much about learning Haida since my mother was hesitant about her own Haida skills. Aside from a few kinship terms, she rarely taught me or my siblings any Haida except an occasional descriptive term, such as *sklunai*, which literally means 'shitty ass'. Years would pass before I would think more about Haida.

In 1990 I began my Master of Arts Degree in Teaching English to Speakers of Other Languages program (MA TESOL). After my first introductory language acquisition course, I became fascinated with the subject. During the completion of my Ph.D. course requirements for the degree in Applied Linguistics, this fascination would ultimately lead me to consider some of the current second language acquisition theories in light of Native American language situations.

In particular, I was very curious to see whether the theories would be applicable. I wrote a paper for John Schumann's language acquisition course comparing his acculturation model for second language acquisition (Schumann 1978) with the historical situation of the New Mexico Tewa learning Spanish (see Dozier 1951) and the Haida learning English. With the caveat that the model's originally intended subjects were immigrants, I suggested that the theory was inadequate when applied to Native American tribes since it could not account for the language learning experiences of the Tewa or the Haida. His concluding comment on the paper was "very interesting." Writing this paper opened my eyes to what was happening with many of the Native American tribes linguistically, and I saw the need for a more relevant approach that accounted for language loss and revitalization. At this point I came across a copy of Philips' article on the Warm Springs Indians (1972a). I knew that it was a key to understanding what I would later ponder concerning Haida language instruction. I began thinking that the concept of unique classroom participation styles was especially relevant for the Haida students learning Haida.

With my interest in Haida rekindled, I asked the Massett Band's Educational Coordinator, Hope Setso, for instructional tapes on Haida. She was not aware of any at that time, though she mentioned that the Haida Gwaii school district had recently implemented Haida lessons in their two elementary schools. She also mentioned that the Haida program might have some employment opportunities concerning curriculum development. This was in early 1993.

In the summer of 1993, the Haida Gwaii School District sought and ultimately hired me as a Curriculum Coordinator for the Haida Language program. It was in this context that I began gathering Haida classroom data. The main reasons for which I collected data were to observe and analyze Haida student interaction in the classroom and to observe the instructors' teaching styles. The first reason served to guide the curriculum development and the latter was for raising the instructors' awareness to improve their teaching effectiveness.

As I began completing my Ph.D. requirements for the degree in Applied Linguistics, I wanted somehow to incorporate some aspect of Haida into my dissertation. With gratitude as my motivation--the Massett Band had funded my education up to the dissertation--I wanted to do something that would benefit the Haida community. I then began to see that I could contribute by doing a dissertation on the Haida language program. I approached the Haida instructors in Skidegate and explained my desire and the proposed scope of the dissertation. They were very interested and agreed to let me do the research. We then approached the principal and explained to her what I wanted to do, and she was also very interested and agreed to let me continue. Thus, with the approval of the Haida instructors and the school principal, I began to collect more data for comparison.

First field work and data collection

During the winter of 1994, I spent 10 days on Haida Gwaii observing and videotaping the Haida classes in both Masset and Skidegate. I divided my time between both locations and spent time informally in both Masset and Skidegate with the elders who were involved in teaching the language. I also informally interviewed the teachers.

My data from this trip comprises approximately four hours of video (K-7) recorded during the first week of January, 1994. This videotaped data is divided almost equally between both locations. I also observed approximately 20 hours of Haida K-7 classroom lessons, again equally divided between Masset and Skidegate. In Masset I also had the opportunity to observe approximately four hours of 6th and 7th grade English (the subject English) classroom lessons.

In addition, I obtained results from two Haida Gwaii School District surveys: a survey which asked parents to respond to various questions concerning their children, including what they thought of the Haida language program; and a student survey which also sampled response to the Haida language classes.

Pondering Philips' work on participation (1972a; 1983), and with this data in hand, I began to explore the possibility that there existed a learning and participation style unique to the Haida. It was also clear that the best venue for such research would be Skidegate since the classrooms there were more integrated than in Masset, which had a dominant Haida population in the classrooms I had observed. The result of the pilot data was the seed that ultimately grew into research for this study.

1996 proposal

At the beginning of the 1996 school year, I went to the teachers in Skidegate with an idea for a project. Essentially, I proposed a project in which we could verify the impact of modifying the teaching to enhance the participation of first grade Haida students. The modifications would include adjustments to the teachers' style which implemented traditional apprenticeship/teacher interaction. The idea was to have one class split in two with one taught without any modifications and the other with the modifications. Both teachers were excited about the project.

We, the two Haida teachers and I, then went to see the principal. I explained to the principal that such a project would be beneficial to all involved on many levels. The principal was very interested and had studied Native American cultural differences in her university training. She also agreed to the proposal. I then explained that I would not be on site but that it was necessary to videotape the class prior to the winter break 1996 and then prior to the spring break 1997. They were to send the data to me after video-taping. However, they never video-taped any of their classes because, as they explained, they were too busy to set the camera up and video-tape as well teach the class.

I had not planned on any videotaping during that trip and subsequently only observed the classroom lessons. I waited for two years to receive the videotape data and by then, the original project had all but been forgotten. I did persuade the vice-principal to record some lessons and she recorded two lessons in June of 1998, only one of which I could transcribe. I then went to secure more data before the winter break in 1998 recording both the Kindergarten and the first grade lessons.

The post-proposal data

In an attempt to secure data to complete my book, I flew to Haida Gwaii during the second week of December 1998. I spent a week with the instructors and recorded approximately 125 minutes of first grade Haida lessons and 45 minutes of Kindergarten lessons. Along with the data the vice-principal had recorded, there is approximately 205 minutes of videotape. I also informally interviewed the teachers, a session which was recorded on a 45 minute audio-tape.

All the recorded data provides at the very least a basis for a preliminary analysis. I cannot expect to do more with the limited data and subsequent analysis will undoubtedly reflect the limitations of my database, though the data has the promise of establishing a solid foundation for extended on-site research.

During that 1998 visitation, the vice-principal also gave me the results of the Provincial Subjects Tests. The data contained the regional scores for English writing and revealed that Haida Gwaii was the lowest in most of the categories. Only in one category did another region, the neighboring Prince Rupert School District 51, score lower.

Audio and video transcription

Transcription is the attempt to put on paper dialogue recorded on audio or videotape. The process involves repetitious listening as well as editing in order to produce a true-to-life representation on paper of such dialogue. Ochs (1979:43) suggests that the transcriber's theoretical presuppositions greatly influence the final product. Included in the process of transcription is symbolic representation of language. It is within the symbolic representations that the process instantiates the transcriber's presuppositions.

An important methodological question concerns how to represent questions, intonation, surprise, or supra-segmental aspects of language such as vowel lengthening, word contractions, or even dialect variations on paper. Other issues concern spelling and punctuation, which are other elements revealing the theoretical bent of the transcriber. The process, therefore, not only produces a transcript, but a theoretically biased product as well. Thus, the results reflect not only recorded linguistic material, but interpolations of the transcriber's ideology concerning issues of language use and even motion, gestures, and facial expressions.

The following transcripts provide the basis of comparison and a discourse analysis in accordance with Duranti (1985:193), Ochs (1979:43), Sachs, Schegloff and Jefferson (1974) in order to investigate student participation styles in the Haida classrooms. For my purposes, I have implemented different levels of detail in my transcriptions in order to address what I thought was important.

I have modified the forms to suit my approach and will use the following conventions in my transcriptions:

1.   words that are in Haida will be italicized, e.g. *guud* (eagle)

2.   English translations of Haida words will follow in single parentheses where necessary, e.g. *guud* (eagle)

3.   lexical items that are unclear will be in double parentheses, e.g. ((snake))

4.   double parentheses also indicate time lapses to the tenth of a second between utterances, e.g.   J: well ((1.4)) okay

5.   descriptions of motion or action will be in curly brackets
   e.g. J: there {pointing to the place}

6.   an upward pointing arrow ↑ indicates rising intonation. I only regarded rising intonation in my transcripts to indicate questioning or inquiry. e.g. F: when did you start↑

7.   underlining and capitalization indicate emphasis and loudness respectively,
   a) e.g. G: <u>boy</u> that's a tough one to remember,
   b) e.g. S: HEY LOOK

8.   colons within a word indicate lexical lengthening, e.g. S: HE::Y

9.   a series of ten periods indicates a break in the sequence of recording,   e.g. . . . .

10.   ": indicates a continuation of the speaker from the previous line,
    e.g.   J: and when we get to the end we will do
    ": a couple more for the holidays

11. I use left brackets [to indicate interruptions and the right brackets] for closure of the sequence, e.g. J: here is the[

S: I can do it

J:]paper

12. Identification of the speakers is done as follows:

a) G and D for the Haida instructors

b) TA indicates the teacher assistant

c) MT indicates the mainstream teacher

d) TA2 indicates the other teacher assistants

e) S represents students and G (girl) or B (boy) indicates respective gender e.g. SG: hey look at my ornament

f) an H beside the speaker indicates that the student is Haida

g) U indicates unison responses

h) Any letter for student names represents direct teacher address

i) ?: indicates an unidentifiable speaker

j) at times it is not possible to identify the students individually, thus, I will number the responses only as different responses and not as different students until the instructor speaks again, eg.

S1: no

S2: wait

S3: look

D: okay

S1: what

k) letters of identified speakers (all the names are pseudonyms as part of the agreement I made with the instructors) will follow respectively, or if the letter is the same as the previous speaker, the first two letters e.g.

G: hey Anita here you go

A: thank you

G: Gail here's yours

Ga: thanks

I analyze the first set of data, Appendices A and B, to establish the fact of distinct Haida participation styles. The analysis focuses on discerning what that style entails and what the students are doing.

I analyze the second set of data in terms of two categories: 1. participation in lessons with little or no Haida; and 2. participation in actual Haida instruction. I want to determine difference in actual participation by separating the two types of lessons and providing a closer analysis of the students in the classroom.

Skidegate students and instructors.

The main focus of the following chapters will be Kindergarten and first grade classrooms in Skidegate. There were approximately 400 students (K-8) enrolled in the school during each year of videotaping.

I had originally asked for the class rosters as well in order to have an accurate record of the students in the class, but I did not obtain any. I was then limited to counting the students I could see on the screen to determine how many students were in the lessons. From time to time it was evident that there may have been more students in the class than what I could see on the screen. Under these conditions, I could only estimate the number of students in each class.

The following chart provides information for the appendices B through F. Appendix A is an excerpt of Appendix B and is not included on the chart. The lessons with an asterisk (*) indicate the lessons that may have had more students than I could see on the screen.

Number of Students

Appendix	Boys	Girls	Haida Boys	Haida Girls	Total Haida	Total Students
B*	5	5	4	3	7	17
C	6	1	0	5	5	12
D*	3	5	3	4	7	15
E	3	4	1	4	5	12
F	5	2	4	3	7	14
G	4	2	4	8	12	18

There are two main Haida instructors in Skidegate: one is a semi-fluent elder (her own evaluation), and an apprentice in her mid-30s. Dora has taught Haida for eight years, only one month less than her apprentice colleague, Genie. They are not certified teachers as of yet, but are trying to attain certification based on the hours that they have already taught in the classroom. Neither has graduated from university.

When discussing my proposal with the instructors, I mentioned to them that I would refer to them by their real names only if they agreed to let me. It was evident they preferred anonymity, thus, we agreed to use pseudonyms rather than their real names.

In Masset, there are four female Haida teachers: a fluent bilingual elder, and three apprentices with varying degrees of proficiency. For both locations, the Haida program began a week later than the regular school program, and ended two weeks earlier.

The Haida classes in both locations were approximately 20-30 minutes for each lesson, with Skidegate having lessons only twice a week. The Skidegate Kindergarten class differed in that the lesson was 20 minutes a day.

Conclusion

I want to approach the analysis of video and audio data with the purpose of noting Haida students' participation styles. In light of Philips' observation that, though there is acknowledgement of distinct learning styles, little effort focuses on teaching methodology adjustments (1983:133), I want to provide a basis for cultural brokerage (Stairs 1993; Kirkness 1998), in which the blending of both the native learning styles and teaching styles meet in a manner that promotes greater Haida participation. My conclusion will address implications of my research and will include suggestions for promoting greater Haida student participation as well as observations on what hinders effective participation.

Chapter 4
The case for Haida participation

Discovering Haida participation styles.

Philips' work (1972a, 1983) presented the notion that the Warms Springs Indians had a style of classroom participation noticeably different from that of their Euro-American classmates. Before long, many others agreed with Philips' idea of distinct classroom learning behavior, including Hayes (1990), Stairs (1992), Swisher (1990), Tafoya (1989), and Wilgosh & Mulcahy (1993), all of whom have also observed that Native Americans do indeed behave and respond differently within the classroom.

In this chapter, I want to apply these ideas of difference in learning and participating to the Haida students. I assume that Haida students participate differently than their fellow Euro-Canadian classmates do. The first set of video data to and the field notes from my observations serve to support my assumption.

In this section, I describe Haida participation styles. The following analysis of approximately three minutes of classroom activity will illustrate these different participation styles. During this period the first grade class has been in session for almost ten minutes. My focus is the Haida students; I am particularly interested in how the Haida students interact with each other and with the instructor, and how this differs from the behavior of their classmates.

My analysis of the first section, the General Class Setting, is an overview and introduction to the main characters: Jason, a Haida student, and the Haida instructor. The discussion centers on how the instructor executes her lesson plan and how most students participate. Particular attention to Jason's pattern of participation segues into the following sections: II. Participation through a plan, and III. Co-construction of participation. In these two sections, I observe and consider Jason's pattern more intricately. In section II, Jason plans and implements his participation, and in section III, with the help of Sara, another student, Jason accomplishes his plan. All words in Haida are italicized and an unspoken translation follows immediately in parentheses-such as with *gyuu* (ear)-after each mention for simplicity. Double parentheses indicate words or phrases that are unclear.

General class setting

The Haida instructors do not have their own classroom, therefore they walk to each classroom when they are scheduled to teach Haida lessons. Each grade (from the first to the seventh grade) has twenty or twenty-five minute lessons twice a week.

A first grade class in Skidegate Elementary School provides the setting for the main analysis. When the mainstream first grade teacher saw the Haida instructor arrive, he announced that it was time for the Haida lesson. He promptly had the students clean up their desks, put away all their materials, and prepare for the Haida lesson.

The Haida lesson plan analyzed here focused on basic Haida vocabulary. The instructor had the students draw pictures for six Haida nouns on a piece of paper sectioned into six compartments. She drew a large rectangle divided into six compartments on the board anticipating student involvement. She planned to have individual students draw pictures of the various nouns in each compartment.

The transcription begins as the instructor asks if the students had finished drawing on their papers and then invites students to draw the words on the board. The six Haida words were: *saablii* (bread), *daaws* (cat), *gyuu* (ear), *xaa* (dog), *na* (house), and *guud* (eagle). A full transcript appears in Appendix B.

In this section, I provide only a preliminary analysis, an overview. The instructor has previously given the six Haida terms for the students to draw, she allows a few minutes to pass, and then she calls for class participation. She begins the sequence with a question.

```
001    D:    Okay, you got it all down↑
002    ":    as much as you can get↑
```

Having allowed a few minutes for the students to work on their own, with this question she clearly transitions from individual desk work with an invitation to group board work. Then as she continues, she indicates her desire for participation at the board,

```
005    D:    and then I get somebody
006    ":    to come up
007    ":    and draw for me  ((OK))
```

She has now transitioned from individual to group participation. Having set the stage for voluntary individual performance, she is immediately barraged with volunteers to help her. Interestingly, only two of the Haida students, Jason and Sara (signified in the transcript with bold H preceding their names) actually participate in this part of the lesson. The competitive setting is not that inviting for the other Haidas, confirming Swisher and Deyhle's comment that the Native students are normally reluctant to participate in a manner that requires being singled out from the whole group (1989:6). Jason and Sara's participation will be considered in greater detail in the following section, but suffice to say here that this preliminary participation changes to more traditional modes of interaction as the lesson unfolds.

Two other Haida students, Charles and Don, in the midst of the lesson, only briefly interact with each other as Charles seemingly wants Don's attention. The interaction stops when Don replies and realizes that Charles wants to give him a pencil. He retrieves the pencil and then goes back to his desk. This interaction seems to substantiate Philips'(1972a:376) and MacAvoy and Sidles' (1991:33) observations concerning first graders' class behavior, notably, failure to conform to classroom procedure, capacity to wander in the middle of the lesson, and greater interest in other students than in the teacher. The remaining Haida students watch the instructor or continue with their drawings.

For the rest of the class, participation is immediate and the students begin by self-assignment or self-selection. They confidently and vocally volunteer or assign themselves to draw a particular noun,

008   Casey: me {hand raised and waving}

009   Ann: I'll do *saablii* (bread)

010   ":   I'll do *saablii*   {hand raised and waving}

011   ":   I'll do *saablii*   {hand raised and waving}

012   Dawn: I'm *guud* (eagle) {hand raised and waving}

013   Hope: I'm *gyuu*. (ear)...oo::hh:: {hand raised and waving}

014   Ann: *saablii*   {hand raised and waving}

The self-selection begins immediately after the instructor mentions that she "will get somebody to come up and draw for me." The competitive nature of the Euro-Canadians even at the first grade level manifests itself as one of the major differences in this Haida classroom. The Haida students are content to watch, but the Euro-Canadian students eagerly and vocally self-assign their involvement.

It is also important to note that at first, the majority of non-Haida students raise and wave their hands, and interestingly, during the hand raising sequence, no Haida students raise or wave their hands. This is significant because Philips (1983:109) noted that the Warm Springs students rarely engaged in hand raising and the Haida students confirm her observation. Raising one's hand has repercussions that are not consistent with native students' comfort level and socialization: it indicates a willingness to be singled out, something the Haidas do not like or want; and displays knowledge in a manner that makes one look better than others, which is unacceptable in most native communities.

From this point on the students then begin to assign themselves a task or ask for permission to participate. The instructor's class management style is not like that of the students' mainstream teacher; the instructor allows greater freedom for the students to participate orally at a level of noise that the mainstream teacher never permits. At the end of the Haida lesson and the beginning of his lesson, he immediately reinstates his authority and management style within in one minute, conforming to the style that Philips (1972a:377) observed in which the oral responses were only given with his approval. With the Haida instructor, the Euro-Canadian students noisily dominate and participate while most of the Haidas draw and quietly color or watch the action on the board. With the mainstream teacher, all interaction and speech is contingent on his approval.

The Haida instructor utilizes various methods of ratification orally and non-verbally. To ratify students responses, or to approve in this case, the instructor gives approval verbally or with gestures. Specifically, she acknowledges student requests with "okay" or a nod of approval while gazing in their direction. In most students' pursuit of participation, the instructor orally acknowledges the students' effort for involvement. But Jason, a Haida student, wants to draw the house, but does not seem convinced that his request to draw the house (*na* in Haida) has been approved/ratified. His actions and further interaction seems to confirm his doubts concerning his participation. The sequence begins with Jason's self-assignment to draw 'house' and the instructor responding immediately,

029	H Jason:	I'll do that house
030	D:	Okay
031	Jane:	I'll do *saablii* (bread)
032	Frank:	I'll do house
033	Jane:	I'll do *saablii*
034	H Jason:	I'm doing house

Jason wants to draw the house, and after his self-assignment, in line 029, he hears the instructor's immediate positive response. Frank, in line 031, also through self-assignment, wants to draw the house as well. Jason responds swiftly in line 034 saying emphatically, "I'm doing house." But, as we consider more of the lesson, Jason is not satisfied that he has settled the issue.

Jason's apparent dissatisfaction with his participation, or approval for participation, manifests itself in his actions. As the lesson continues, he plans and secures his participation by gaining permission face-to-face with the instructor (lines 054-068) rather than by sitting at his desk and vocalizing his desire like most of his Euro-Canadian classmates. He gets up from his desk and as he walks toward her, he calls her name,

054   H Jason:] Dora↑ (0.5) Dora↑ [

055   ":   ] [Dora, can I do the house↑

056   ":   ]{walking to the instructor}

Only the Haida instructors allow their students to call them by their first name, all the other mainstream teachers insist on the obligatory titles "Mr." or "Ms." and their last names. Here, Jason is free to address her as Dora. Having reached her side, Jason asks the question, but others entreat the instructor with questions as well,

057 Jane: can I do *saablii* ↑ (bread)

058 H Jason: can [I do the house↑

059 ":   ]{standing beside the blackboard gazing at the instructor}

060 D: okay, uhmm {watching the board}

061 ":   {glances twice at the boy}

062 Jane: ((can I do bread)) ↑

063 ":   can I do *saablii* ↑

064 ":   can I do *saablii* ↑

065 ":   can I do *saablii*↑

066 ":   can I do *saablii*↑

067 H Jason: I get to do hou:se[

068 ":   ]{turns around and goes back to his seat}

In this sequence, Dora provides evidence of approval (line 060), which apparently satisfies Jason. After seemingly securing permission to participate, Jason makes his way back to his desk. He has secured his right to participate and sits down to wait for his turn to draw the house.

In summary, the general setting reveals minimal participation from Haida students; in fact, Jason is the only Native American student who competes to participate on the board. When he does participate, he does so in a way different from the Euro-Canadian students. As the instructor implements her methods of ratification, the students are usually acknowledged orally, though nonspecifically, and physically through a nod. Jason, seemingly, is not comfortable with the nonspecific ratification and seeks face-to-face ratification in order to secure his participation in the lesson. The following sections explicate the contrastive nature of Jason's action in light of Native American classroom participation.

Participation through planning

In the middle of the lesson, Jason's participation becomes overtly intentional. But he pursues his desire to participate quite differently from his Euro-Canadian classmates. Seemingly requiring more confirmation for his participation, Jason develops and executes a plan to secure his participation. My purpose in considering the following expanded portion of transcript provides the basis for analyzing the progression of the plan in which Jason exemplifies Native American patterns for classroom behavior. According to Ochs (1994), a plan is a type of narrative centered on an unresolved event or circumstance of past, present, future, or hypothetical significance. A narrative, according to Labov (1972), is a combination of elements of which comprises a "narrative structure." These elements are: abstract, orientation, complicating action, evaluation, result or resolution, and coda (Labov 1972:362). Thus, for Jason, the important elements of a plan include a complicating action, evaluation, and resolution in an attempt to confront and resolve a problem.

Jason's predicament is that he is not convinced that his desire to participate in drawing the house has been secured. His desire to draw the house thus motivates him to plan his participation because his previous self-assignment apparently does not provide him with the confidence that he needs. He executes a plan, then, to secure his participation, as seen in the following transcript sections and subsequent analysis.

As the plan sequence begins, the instructor responds to a Euro-Canadian student's inquiry. At this juncture, Jason initiates face-to-face contact with the instructor.

053	D:	]okay [{to inquiring student}
054	H Jason:	] Dora↑ (0.5) Dora↑ [
055	":	[{walking to the instructor}]
056	":	] Dora, can I do the house↑

As this portion of the transcript begins, the instructor supplies feedback to another student before Jason's request and his initial development of the plan. Jason begins his efforts by calling the instructor's name three times before he asks his question. He is also walking towards her as he calls her name.

Jason plans to secure his participation for drawing on the board, and he proceeds by asking the instructor for permission by walking up to ask her face-to-face for permission to draw the house. Philips (1983:121) mentions that a typical strategy to get attention for Warm Springs students was to wait until a reading or desk assignment, then raise their hands for one-on-one interaction, or to go to the teacher and ask her face-to-face. Jason's actions confirm Philips's observations in this class as well. Jason does not compete for the Haida instructor's attention in the same manner as all the other students; instead, he addresses the Haida instructor face-to-face and establishes eye contact with her. Swisher and Deyhle (1989:6) note reluctance in being singled out for participation, so, instead of raising his hand and being singled out, and thus drawing the attention of the class to himself, Jason prefers face-to-face interaction.

Jason's plan for participation meets with some competition for the instructor's attention from the other students. As Jason stands there, Jane's questions are incessant and loud. After her initial effort (line 057), she resorts to the English and asks if she can "do bread" (line 062), then asks four more times using Haida *saablii* (lines 063-067). The instructor does not respond to her, but in the middle of the sequence, immediately after Jason's question, she says "okay..uhmm" (line 060), but it is not clear whether this response is to Jason's request or to Jane's. Since Jane is not satisfied that it is a positive response to her quest, she continues to ask the question. Jason, on the other hand, walks back to his desk with sing-song confidence stating "I get to do house."

In this section, Jason stands close to the instructor and awaits her approval for his participation. Twice the instructor turns to Jason and gazes at him. She also says okay to his request to draw the house. Ultimately, his effort culminates in a confident statement. Jason is satisfied that he got what he wanted and sits down. Philips observes that eyebrow raising among some Native Americans indicates "yes" (1988:157), and though it is not possible to see the instructor that well on the screen, this also may account for Jason's sense of approval. His plan seems secure, though it would be challenged shortly.

Jason's response is one of confidence as he states line 067 in a sing-song fashion. He has obtained the instructor's ratification, and thus, partially completed his plan for securing his participation. Thus, he has seemingly solved his problem of participation through a series of face-to-face questions. The instructor's vocal response satisfies Jason's need for permission to draw the house. But as the lesson continues, Jane thwarts his plan for participation. In section III, Jane challenges Jason's plan and the result is a triadic co-construction of Jason's participation. Jason's efforts ultimately culminate in participation, but not as he initially wants.

Co-constructing participation

Co-construction here refers to efforts of two or more interlocutors involved in discourse "building." It is the process or means of securing an end, which, in this case, is classroom participation. In this section, Jason's desire to draw the house is thwarted by Jane, whose indirect role is also important. She has been very vocal throughout the lesson, initially wanting to draw *saablii* (bread), but which the instructor assigns to someone else. Even after not securing permission to draw *saablii*, Jane is still determined to draw something, and seeks to draw *na* (house). Jason has secured permission to draw the house, which is *na*, but he used the English term and not the Haida word. Jane receives permission to draw *na* (house), and as she begins drawing, a triadic co-construction of participation for Jason follows. The Haida instructor, Jason and Sara work together to address Jason's situation.

This sequence then models a co-construction of participation for Jason though he does not say anything until the end of the sequence. Sara, the Haida instructor, and Jason provide the co-construction through an interesting triadic interaction.

Jane initiates the sequence of co-construction by a face-to-face request to draw the house. She is not a participant in the co-construction of Jason's participation, but her actions instigate his ultimate involvement in drawing on the board. Perhaps noticing how Jason obtained permission, Jane copies his effort by dealing with the instructor face-to-face. She is very quiet in this sequence, in contrast to her previous clamorous attempts to participate. As she quietly catches the instructor's attention, she asks timidly for permission to draw *na* (house).

105   Jane: Dora, can I ((do/draw)) the *na* (house)

106   D: okay {points to the board}

107   Jane: {goes to the board and draws a house}

It is interesting to note that this is the first time in this part of the lesson that this Haida noun, *na* (house) appears. Jason in his attempts at participation, has referred only to the English term thus far. The instructor approves Jane's request, and she immediately begins to draw the house. Her movement to the board does not go unnoticed, which then begins the triadic co-construction of Jason's participation.

Sara notices Jane drawing the house and immediately asks the instructor what she is doing. At this juncture a dyadic co-construction of Jason's participation begins between the instructor and Sara.

108 H Sara: ((what is she drawing/doing))

109   D: She is doing *na* (house) right now

110   ":   {looking at Jane and pointing at Jane /board}

111 H Jason: {stands up}

112 H Sara: Jason's doing that

113   D: O::h I forgot Jason's supposed to do house

As soon as Sara sees Jane drawing something, she seeks clarification of Jane's action.   Upon confirmation that Jane is drawing the house, Sara immediately reminds the instructor that Jason has previously obtained permission to draw the house.

The sequence is rather intriguing in terms of instructor ratification of student requests.   Jane wants to draw *na* (house), which the instructor approves. Sara, seeing Jane drawing the house, seeks clarification about Jane's action.   The instructor responds to Sara that Jane was drawing *na* (house).   But when Sara reminds the instructor that "Jason's doing that," the instructor immediately responds that she has forgotten that she had given Jason approval to draw the house.   Using the same term that Jason had used throughout this phase of the lesson, she uses the English term for the first time, "I forgot Jason's supposed to do house."   In fact, it is only the third time in this sequence that she has used English terms for the Haida nouns she wants drawn.   But it is the first time she has said this particular term in English, and she uses it as Jason did.   Both students receive ratification for the terms that they used, though the terms are for one and the same noun.   The problem now facing the instructor is to remedy Jason's situation.

The instructor then attempts to co-construct a remedy with Sara and Jason for Jason's participation.

114 H Jason: {begins to walk up front but stops at the desk}

115   D: Hey, Jason {bends down to look at the board}

116 H Sara: Jason

117   D: Jason can you draw me a *gyuu* [= (ear)

60

118   ":   ]{looks at Jason}

Jason has left his desk and silently watches Jane draw the house as the instructor tries to see what other nouns remain to be drawn. Seguin (1988:147) notes that Native Americans' silence can represent a challenge and certainly Jason's silence in this phase indicates his challenge. The instructor calls his name as she tries to include him in the lesson. Sara immediately echoes his name as the co-construction of Jason's participation continues. The instructor then substitutes *gyuu* (ear) for house and asks Jason if he could draw the *gyuu*. This is a change in the sequence as all other assignments are student initiated, but here, in order to appease Jason and correct her mistake, the instructor asks Jason if he wants to draw the ear. She has come up with an alternative way for Jason to participate, and now it is Jason's turn to interact in the co-construction.

Jason stands watching Jane and the instructor as he listens to Sara and the instructor. His action seems to suggest a desire to participate, even though he has been silent thus far. But in this case Jason seems to embody the cliché, "actions speak louder than words," as this section reveals,

119 H Jason: {begins walking to the board}
120   D: then *gyuu*, for ear, can you do that {stands erect}
121 H Sara: ((you got to spell house though) {comments to Jane}
122   ":   {provides the letters} o....u....s....e
123 H Jason: {goes to the board and looks and finds chalk}
124   ":   [yeah I'll draw *gyuu* (ear)
125   ":   ]{putting a finger in his ear as he draws}

Jason's assent to drawing the ear can immediately be seen by his walking to the board. His silence does not necessarily mean a challenge here, but rather a refusal to have attention drawn to himself as he stands in front of the class. The instructor seeks ratification of the co-construction and uses both terms instead of just the Haida for clarity. During Jason's silence, Sara instructs Jane to write the English translation for *na* and provides her with the letters. Jason, finally walks to the board, orally responds to the instructor, "yeah," and begins to draw an ear. The fact that he responds at the board suggests to me that it is safer to respond when he can focus on the board and not have anyone see his face. Any attention drawn to him while he is up front can easily be ignored as he focuses on his task.

The co-construction is successful, and as this portion of the class ends, the instructor takes the time to acknowledge Jason's participation.

126 D: That's a good ear {commenting on Jason drawing}

127 ":   ((1.2) that's a re::al good ear

Interestingly, there are only a few times during this lesson in which the instructor openly comments on the participation of the students drawing on the board. In her comments, she has said "good" or "good job" to two of the other students, but with Jason, she is very explicit. She specifically addresses his drawing, not once, but twice with a vocally inflected intensifier, "real," the second time. Her comments to Jason seem to ratify the fact that he is the only Native American student participating in drawing the Haida nouns and her words serve to provide encouragement for that effort.

Summary

In sum, the co-construction that evolved concerns the ratification of Jason's desire to draw the house on the board, as well as his desire for participation. In the middle of the lesson, Jane approaches the instructor and asks if she can draw *na* (house). The instructor approves and Jane goes to the board and begins to draw. Sara, aware that Jason has previously volunteered himself to draw the house, brings the instructor's attention to the problem. The instructor immediately acknowledges that Jason was supposed to do the house and endeavors to resolve the problematic situation. Her resolution of the problem is to have Jason draw the *gyuu* (ear).

The scene is fast and very fascinating as Jason's right to draw the house is also verified by another student, Sara, as well as by the instructor. Interestingly, Jason does not interfere with Jane as she draws the house, nor does he say anything to her or to the instructor during the sequence until the instructor finishes solving the problem. Jason's silence may be indicative of a pattern of participation consistent with some Native American students, which is not to highlight a problem but to seek satisfaction for being wronged. He silently stands, watches, listens, and waits for further instructions. Justice prevails when Jason receives a substitute for 'house' and finally draws an ear which is then validated by the instructor.

Earlier, Jason had requested to draw the house and was seemingly given the right to do so. Jane's effort to draw the house reflects an interesting interaction because in subsequent discussion it was the first time in the lesson that the instructor referred to any of the vocabulary in English, and it is the same and only word that Jason previously had requested in English. Thus, she ratifies Jason's right to do the house and acknowledges that she had given him the permission to do so. Her accommodation in providing another noun for him to draw also affirms Jason's right to draw something. Because he has initially secured the right earlier and has been thwarted by Jane, the instructor provides an alternative way for Jason to participate legitimately.

Jason's acknowledgment of a problem begins as he hears the instructor respond to Sara, and he rises from his seat and makes his way to the front of the classroom. He does not say anything, but looks at the instructor and the board and then stands there as the instructor provides the solution to the problem. His agreement is not immediately vocalized though he grabs the chalk and then finally he says "Yeah, I'll draw *gyuu* (ear)." As he draws the ear, he is ratified and encouraged by the instructor's comments, such as "That's a good ear," and later "That's a real good ear!".

Discussion

In the general overview, I introduced the class setting and the four main characters: Jason, Sara, Jane, and the instructor. The Haida students in the general setting revealed interesting conformity to Philips' observation of the

Warm Spring Indians, such as when much of the class had raised their hands, no Haidas had their hands raised. Don and Charles also exemplified Philips' observation of a lack of interest in what the teacher was doing (1973:391) by wandering around in the middle of the lesson (1973:376). There was only minimal Haida participation in the vying for permission to draw on the board. Jason's attempt to participate through planning reveals a cultural preference for face-to-face contact, again confirming Philips's observation of Warm Springs Indians student preferences (1983:40).

Jason's perception of ratification is twice confirmed, once by the instructor and once by a Haida classmate. In the co-construction of participation, Jason's participation was culturally very passive and silent. He ultimately provided vocal agreement to draw another noun rather than what he had originally requested, and though he finally participated, it was not what he had originally planned.

Conclusion.

I have endeavored to introduce the idea of Haida participation styles through analysis of an event in a first grade class. Jason's situation not only indicates different participation styles but also illustrates tendencies similar to Philips' observations. Thus, with the notion that there is a Haida participatory style comparable to what Philips observed on the Warm Springs Indian Reservation (1972a; 1983), in the next chapter, utilizing Philips' notion of participant structures (1972b; 1982), I will extend my analysis of the Haida students' participation style in greater detail.

Chapter 5

Looking more closely at the Haida Lessons

Introduction

My intention in this chapter is to analyze two types of Haida lessons: Firstly, lessons in which there is little or no Haida language instruction; and secondly, lessons in which there is a significant amount of Haida language instruction. By significant, I mean time when the instructors actually focused on teaching Haida. In the transcripts, these lessons have at least a third of the class lesson time focused on Haida language instruction.

My interest in examining the classroom based on these two types of lessons is to identify in greater detail what Haida students are doing in each situation. We also need to consider how the mainstream teachers and students define the time spent with the Haida instructors. The following section addresses the definition of Haida lessons and the subsequent sections examine the transcripts.

Defining Haida lessons.

What is a Haida lesson? Even though there may be little or no Haida spoken, the general consensus among the instructors, the mainstream teachers, and even the students is that when the Haida instructors are in the classroom, what is happening is a Haida lesson. What constitutes a 'Haida' lesson? The answer seems to be that the Haida instructors' presence implies a Haida lesson. There is no specific guideline or requirement for Haida content. When Christmas or Easter holidays approach, the instructors usually take the lesson time to make crafts and forego Haida language instruction.

Comments from mainstream teachers are cited to illustrate the attitude they have towards the Haida lessons. The first excerpt (from Appendix C) reveals the mainstream teacher's sense of dissociation from the Haida lessons. In this lesson, the students are preparing Christmas ornaments to hang on their Christmas trees. Some students are wandering around the class as the mainstream teacher tells the students,

224 MT: you guys go and sit down and do your Haida stuff

even though the mainstream teacher is doing a similar activity as the students, a Christmas related craft. She later adds to her comment in order to emphasize that the ornaments are currently the Haida lesson,

229 MT: When you finish your Haida ornaments here's a Christmas coloring
230 ":   contest but you have to finish your Haida ornaments first.

Though both are craft focused, the Haida crafts must be finished first before the mainstream teacher allows the students to start her coloring contest.

In another excerpt (from Appendix B), the Haida lesson is nearly finished. The vocabulary lesson, writing six Haida terms on a piece of paper and drawing pictures for each term, *saablii* (bread), *daaws* (cat), *gyuu* (ear), *xaa* (dog), *na* (house) and *guud* (eagle), allows some students to finish faster than others, depending on the detail they have in their illustrations. Two boys decide they would play a board game since they have completed their drawing and vocabulary writing exercise. At this point, the mainstream teacher reprimands students for trying to begin a game during their Haida lesson noting their Haida lesson time is nearly finished,

337 MT: there's no time for board games ((0.6)) there's no time for
338   ":   board games because Haida finishes in about two minutes.

He hesitates slightly and repeats himself as he interrupts their attempt to play a game. He does not want the children to be playing games when the Haida lesson is over and *then* have to end their game; thus, he stops them from even beginning the game. The impression is that such games could be played during Haida, but not when Haida is over. It seems it is better to deal with the students by stopping them before their Haida lesson ends rather than to confront them on his own time.

Finally, the students themselves understand the presence of the Haida instructors as time spent having Haida lessons. In an excerpt from Appendix C, a student has just come in late. She has, in fact, missed the whole lesson. One of the students promptly comments to her "you missed you missed Haida" (line 290). Though the late student did not respond, it was clear that the time spent making Haida Christmas ornaments with the Haida instructors was actually Haida, not Haida class, nor a Haida lesson, but simply Haida.

Thus, whether or not the lesson actually has Haida language instruction is unimportant. What is important is that the students have time with the Haida instructors. The Haida instructors' presence is what constitutes Haida lessons, regardless of whether or not they teach the Haida language. Perhaps more precisely, the mainstream teachers and students see Haida as a subject and that whatever the Haida instructors do or teach ultimately is Haida regardless of whether or not there is language instruction.

Coloring, cutting and making crafts.

It is important to note that the content of the craft lessons provides limitations on the generalized list of participation style elements and its application to the students. Since they are making individual crafts, much of the learning time focuses on the product they are trying to finish. If they had had to collaborate with each other and then discuss their ideas with the instructor before they began making their crafts, the dynamics certainly would have been different. Or if the instructor had singled a student out to show his or her work to the whole class, the situation would have ensured more typical responses. Thus, the list of participation style elements on pages 18-21 is much more relevant in the Haida language instruction lessons rather than when they are doing the crafts.

To begin with the craft lessons, mainly coloring and making Christmas tree ornaments, the first item, participating at their own discretion, reflects an interesting dynamic in the classroom, that of the Native American student deciding whether or not to participate. For most teachers, this is a very problematic issue (see Philips 1972a:378; Wolcott 1974:413), because the western approach assumes and requires participation regardless of student preference. And even within a setting that is not competitive or does not demand a display of knowledge, such as coloring and doing crafts, the students do not uniformly participate. The student's lack of participation results in the instructor addressing the student by name concerning his or her actions. The following excerpt from Appendix C exemplifies two Haida students not participating as others are. In previous unrelated incidences, both Dallas and Donald have been reprimanded for their behavior. In this sequence, they are now misbehaving together as both Dora and Genie scold them:

255 D: Dallas and Donald sit down and color put those away HEY
256 G: Donald did you finish yet↑
257 D: DALLAS AND DONALD Dallas that's the 4th time I'm talking to you
258 DoH: and me
259 D: and you
260 G: {walking from the back of the class} yeah and get me mad
261 ": real soon
262 D: color nice pictures we want to laminate them so you take them home

It is near the end of the lesson and perhaps Dallas and Donald are tired of the lesson, but, as the instructor points out, it is the fourth time that she has had to talk to Dallas. Therefore, this was not an isolated incident. At that point, Donald admits it was his fourth time as well. Finally, Genie comes in and threatens to be angry as Dora explains why they want them to finish their crafts so they can take them home.

In this next excerpt, from Appendix E, the students have had a short Haida review. They count from one to ten, sing two songs, and have a short vocabulary drill. For the remaining two thirds of the lesson, the students focus on finishing Christmas crafts. In this excerpt, a student has been playing with some markers, joining them together to the point that they are almost as tall as he is. He should have been coloring his craft, but instead he is making a tall stack of markers:

203 SB: whoa {commenting on his stack of markers} look how many I have
204 TA: finished↑

With this invitation, the class attention draws towards him. Not everyone is as impressed as he is with his accomplishment.

His open invitation for all to see his stack also catches the TA's attention, and she asks him whether or not he has completed his craft. She then works on getting him to join the others in the craft session,

208 TA: come on let's color {dismantling the tower of markers}
209 SBH: I used permanent ((markers)) for that
210 TA: no you started with crayons Genie wants you to finish with crayons OK↑
211 SBH: look
212 TA: all these color then we cut them out and finish them then we can start r
213 ": another one OK↑

Not wanting to color, or perhaps preferring to color in a different way than the instructor preferred, he tries to dodge the TA's request to color by answering that he needs the markers to color. The TA then repeats what the instructions are and encourages him to finish in order to start another craft when he completes the task.

In this particular lesson, this student is the only one who does not readily do what the instructor wants. That he is the only one not willingly participating may seem remarkable, but the instructor's earlier priming of the rest of students for participation and completion of the task could be the reason for an almost unified participation. She begins the crafts session by commenting:

120 G: oh okay well we're going to continue on with our decorations so we can get

121 ": em done because I probably won't see you all next week you'll all be so busy

She addresses the necessity to finish due to time limitations, and almost all the students comply with her request. Shortly thereafter, the instructor also speaks to the tendency of some students wandering as she reminds the students:

150 G: remember we need to stay in our own spot in our space

Thus, she not only encourages everyone to participate, but she also makes sure they color, cut and paste all at their own desk, thereby eliminating any propensity to wander.

The next issue concerns Native American student preference for group oriented tasks. Le Brasseur and Freark comment that there is a notable partiality among Native American students for group work (1982:9). Wolcott also notes that these students commit themselves to greater interaction when they are in small peer groups (1974:414). This excerpt, from Appendix C, shows the interaction of two female Haida students with the instructor as they prepare for the lesson:

1   J: go ahead you'll see it sitting in [

2   SHG:]which office↑

3   SG: Ben

4   SHG: can I go with her↑

5   J: pardon↑

6   SHG: I can help her↑

7   G: sure

8   SHG: I know where they are

9   G: you know what the pencil case looks like↑ you'll see them in our

10   ":   mailboxes the teacher's mailboxes {girls leave the room}

11   ":   girls {leaving the room} in Pam's office

As the lesson begins, the girls volunteer to be helpful by going to get materials from the office together in lines 2, 4, 6, and 8. They do so by face-to-face request for permission (list item 3), the favored mode of interacting with the teacher (Browne 1990:30). The Haida instructor seems to ratify their desire by giving the permission that they want in lines 7, 9, and 10. Later, when they return, the instructor is very pleased as she comments:

40 G: good gee you girls are smart ((2.0)) {taking the pencils from the girls}

thereby affirming their efforts. They have begun the lesson cooperatively and have also been recognized for their participation.

Later in the same transcript, the instructor queries the students for ideas on how to decorate the bulletin board. She then casually invites their suggestions. In this excerpt, she has asked the question "what should I put on you guys' tree?" and they begin supplying their suggestions:

57 S: a stocking

58 SGH: a snowman

59 G: oh I already did a snowman something different

60 S: I know

61 SBH: a Santa Claus

62 G: okay a Santa Claus and a what↑

63 S1:   and reindeer

64 S2:   yeah

65 SBH: yeah

66 G: no a tiny reindeer

67 S1:   I'm Santa he's a reindeer

68 S2:   he's big

69 G: I love these ((1.0)) I missed Alexis

70 SBH: I'll tell you what I am I'm a toy soldier

71 G: yeah you should put a toy soldier on it

72 S1:   yeah

73 S2:   no

74 S3:   yeah

75 G: put a small soldier

76 S: no

77 G: on one and on the other

78 S: I just did an elephant

In this section, almost all the students freely offer answers. Though some Native American students tend to be quiet during a teacher-student information exchange (Swisher and Deyhle 1989), the Haida instructor does not ask for knowledge display, but rather an opinion about what should go on the tree. Thus, there is freedom to provide a suggestion. The result is the free flow of responses from almost all the students, including three replies from Haida students (lines 58, 61, 70). Interestingly, though the last comment from the Haida student in line 70 is not a direct proposal for a Christmas tree ornament, Genie willingly receives his comment as a suggestion.

One final note concerns the instructor's manner of requesting or suggesting, which is different from a typical western teaching approach as well. Since she does not talk with the intention of singling anyone out, the normal western approach, she is open to any comment or answer and the students are aware that anyone who wants may answer. Thus, from the context, it is very clear that the request for suggestions for the bulletin board is not a competitive invitation, but an inclusive one. The instructor invites any or all to comment and does not require students to respond.

Finally, in this last excerpt, found in Appendix D, the instructor has noticed throughout the lesson that a student is not coloring anything or making any crafts. Her comment to the student comes at the end of the lesson and she comments not with reproach or anger, but rather with a sense of empathy as she asks:

164 D: are you lazy today↑

165 Sg: {nods sheepishly}

The instructor then continues walking around without responding any further. She does not reprimand or coax the student to do anything, but accepts the student's decision not to participate.

These excerpts ultimately come from lessons or parts of lessons originally intended for individual work, but situations arose that created opportunities for collaboration (the two girls getting the pencils) and group responses (about filling the bulletin board). Plank suggests that in such environments, Native American students benefit more from a collaborative learning environment (Plank 1994:3) than a competitive one.

A closer look at lessons with Haida instruction.
Item qualifications

To begin this section, I want to comment on my approach. I will examine Appendices E, F, and G and glean from each transcript excerpts to exemplify adherence to or deviation from the Native American student characteristic list. I will consider each characteristic and compare it with the data on each transcript.

There are some characteristics that I can demonstrate through the data I have, and others that are not reflected in the data. This is especially true of the third item, preference for face-to-face interaction, especially since the lessons were such that it was not possible to approach the instructor during this time without having the attention of all the students as well. The sixth item, that Native American students are spatially oriented, seems better demonstrated in lessons that are craft oriented rather than language oriented, perhaps due to the dominant use of the visual modality as well as the constructive element involved with making crafts.

The seventh characteristic, preference for holistic approaches, is difficult to discuss concerning Haida language instruction. The main reason for the difficulty is my lack of quantitative data. In order to observe this item, the teaching methodology would have to include a greater perspective on the subject with an idea of where the students are and where they will be at the end of the year. The ultimate embodiment of the holistic approach for the instructors would have its foundation in their curriculum and ongoing curriculum development. Though this limitation is evident, mainly due to my lack of data, the instructors do embody some holistic methods, for example engaging in song and Total Physical Response (see Asher 1977), a language teaching approach requiring physical responses from students, such as touching their body parts for the song "Head and shoulders, knees and toes" (for a discussion on TPR storytelling as a tool for developing fluency in Native American languages, see Cantoni 1999).

The eighth item, being more interested in other students than in the instructor, does not seem to apply here either. The nature of the Haida instruction is such that the students' attention is quite focused on the lesson. There are gaps or lulls that provide opportunity for students to call out to other students, but during the actual lesson, the students are quite attentive to the language activity. Students may become boisterous as the lessons proceed, but there are few incidents or interruptions due to students seeking fellow students' attention during Haida instruction as opposed to when they were doing crafts. For example, the lesson from Appendix B is a Haida lesson. The main focus was not the Haida language per se, but drawing the nouns and writing the words in Haida. In this case, there were many examples of students talking to others during the lesson, but the nature of the lesson was not Haida instruction focused as much as it was craft focused.

The last item, wandering around the class, proved impossible to illustrate since the structure of the language instruction did not afford the students any freedom to wander at will. The instructors controlled the lessons in such a way that neither face-to-face interaction nor wandering was possible. Thus, with the limited data analyzed, I have only negative evidence of wandering specifically during the Haida language instruction lesson.

Analyzing and comparing the list

The first characteristic concerns participation at the discretion of the student. It is both discretion to participate and not to participate that I want to discuss: perhaps the best indication for both would be doing or responding as the instructor requires or not doing anything or not responding at all. The lesson in Appendix F has two different activities. For the first activity, the students have had to memorize Haida vocabulary for the pictures that they had in front of them. The excerpt here reveals a positive collective responsive to the instructor's question:

117 G: okay now what do you have↑

118 Ss: *kud hlk'aat'aajii* (fence) *tsii kultaxun* (mosquito) *ngaal* (seaweed)

119 ":   *sgaanaa* (orca) *tluu* (canoe) *kaayts'aaw* (star) *tluu* (canoe)

120 ":   *hlguun* (skunk cabbage) *tsiinaa* (salmon) *kinxan* (tree)

The instructor has asked for an answer and it does not seem competitive, which is perhaps why there is such a positive response from most of the students. This activity also embodies opportunities for Haida students to conform to item 13, which refers to Native American students' preference for non-competitive learning. The overlap of items 1 and 13 seem natural as the Haida instructor provides an atmosphere that allows not only discretionary participation, but a non-competitive learning environment.

Another example of willing participation comes later in the same transcript. The instructor has asked what other picture was missing and a student incorrectly responded:

166 G: ahh *gaam* (no) *sgaanaa* (orca) is right here we're missing one more

167 S: fence

168 G: what is the Haida name for fence↑

169 Ss: {look at her but no one answers}

170 G: *kud hlk'aat'aajii*
171 Ss: *kud hlk'aat'aajii* (fence)

A second student provides the correct English answer but the instructor wants the Haida word in line 168. When no one can provide the answer, she provides the answer and they all immediately echo her answer in line 171. The instructor's opened ended query seems less competitively based and the students all willingly repeat the word. This particular activity also exemplifies item 13, participating in activities that are not competitively structured. Researchers find that students are more apt to participate in lessons that are not competitive as opposed to lessons that require rivalry with their peers (LeBrasseur & Freark 1982:9: Shutiva 1991:37).

    A further example comes from Appendix G, the Kindergarten class containing of all Haida students. Here in this excerpt, the students exemplify participation at their own discretion (see Philips 1972:378; Wolcott 1974:413):

82 G: what's this called Angela↑
83 A: {does not answer}
84 Ss: ((*SWANSA*)) ((*SWANSA*)) ((*SWANSA*))
85 G: OHH {makes a zipping motion across her lips in response to noise}
86 Ss: {begin to be quiet}
87 G: uhm Green table what's this one↑ {looks at the back table and points at the
88 ":   third illustration}
89 Ss: ((*SWANSA*))
90 G: GREEN TABLE {looking to her right}
91 Ss: ((*swansa*))
92 G: GREEN TABLE {looking at students directly in front of her}
93 Ss: ((*swansa*))
94 G: {disoriented looking at the tables} ((1.9)) GREEN TABLE {motioning to
95 ":   the students to her left who were the group at the green table}

96 GT: *((swansa))*

Beginning with line 82, the instructor asks Angela for an answer and gets no response from her. Many students do respond willingly with the right answer and it becomes too loud for the instructor to bear so she motions for them to be quiet (line 85}. Perhaps it is because Angela is singled out that she does not respond, but as the class grows too loud, the instructor's attention focuses on regaining control of the class.

Genie then decides on a more general approach and decides to ask one table at a time. This option does not single any one student out, but allows those at the table to respond at their discretion. Interestingly, she asks the green table to respond but keeps on pointing out the wrong table. Though asking the green table specifically to respond (lines 87, 90, and 92), each time she points to the wrong table, and the students at that table willingly give the answer as the green table sits quietly and watches. It is not until the instructor realizes where the green table is that she then asks them and they respond. They allow the other tables to answer the instructor without offering any challenge or correction, but when the instructor finally pinpoints them, they responded just as willingly.

The next point to discuss is the students'enjoyment of group tasks. This particular item refers to situations in which the students can work with others in specified groups, or as a whole. One of the most effective ways to have group participation is to sing a song. The following excerpt from Appendix E reveals the class singing in unison (U):

64 G: great now let's do *dup'juu 7ul'juu* all together again okay
65 U: *dup'juu 7ul'juu yang a jing* (the tiny little spider)
66 ": {making hand motions for a spider}
67 ": went up the *gondl* (water) spout
68 ": {making crawling hand motions up in the air}
69 ": down came the *daala* (rain)

70 ": {making rain falling motions with their hands and fingers}

71 ": and washed the *yang a jing* (spider)

72 ": {making washing motions with their hands}

73 ": out came the *xaaya* (bubbles)

74 ": {making motions for bubbles with their hands to the sky}

75 ": and *gaagaa* all the *daala*

76 ": {making hand motions drying}

77 ": the *dup'juu 7ul'juu yang a jing* (little spider) went up the spout again

78 ": {making motions with their hands to indicate a spider climbing the spout}

Everyone sings the song though not all the students remember the motions. In fact, the instructor watches the students for the first few lines before she actually joins in the motions for the song. Their lively singing and demonstration of the motions for the song reflect the students' enjoyment of tasks that are group oriented.

Perhaps a good indicator of enjoyment is laughter. Laughter usually follows or is part of activities that the children enjoy. There are only 13 students in the following transcript, from Appendix F, as well as the instructor. Engaging in a Total Physical Response activity, the students are enjoying themselves:

29 Ss: {boisterous and laughing} ((12.3))

30 G: okay uhh *gaaw uu hlaa* (sit)

31 Ss: {still laughing as they sit down}

32 G: okay uhh *gaaxaa hlaa* (stand)

33 Ss: {students stand up}

34 G: *gaaw uu hlaa* (sit)

35 Ss: {students sit down}

36 G: *gaaxaa hlaa* (stand)

37 Ss: {students stand up }

38 G: *kunjuu* (sneeze)

39 Ss: atchoo {pretend to sneeze}

40   G: *gaaw uu hlaa* (sit)

41   Ss: {children sit down }

42   G: *gaaxaa hlaa* (stand)

43   Ss: {students stand up }

44   G: *kaa kaa* (walk)

45   Ss: {pretend to walk in place}

Having completed the singing and movements to a Total Physical Response (TPR) song, the children are laughing as they willingly transition to another TPR activity. The TPR approach to learning languages suggests that actions can positively affect learning and remembering language. They all follow the lead of the instructor and seem to like the activity. In sum, they benefit more from group interaction as the instructors engage in a collaborative learning approach (Plank 1994:3).

The fourth characteristic, preferring verbal participation when comfortable with the topic, is perhaps best seen when the instructor asks opened ended questions rather than singling out students for response. This example, from Appendix E, reveals the positive effect of open-ended queries:

79 G: good who remembers how to say dog in Haida↑

80 S: *xaa*

81 G: *xaa* good what about cat↑

82 S: *daaws*

83 G: *daaws* what about cow↑

84 S: *moosmoos*

85 G: what about horse↑

86 S: *gyuudan*

87 G: what about crab↑

88 S: *k'uustan*

89 G: what about frog↑

90 S: *sgaaniinaa*

91 MT: OK yeah

92 G: what about butterfly↑

93 SBH: *kulgaayuugwang*

94 G: good *kulgaayuugwang* <u>boy</u> that's a tough one to remember what about shrimp↑

95 SBH: *guudgaagiigaayd*

96 G: good what about pig↑

97 S: *kobra*

98 G: what about eagle↑

99 S: *xuuya*

100 G: what about eagle↑

101 S: *xuuya*

102 S: what about↑

103 G: what is eagle↑

104 S: *guud*

105 G: what is raven↑

106 SGH: *xuuya*

107 S: snake

108 G: what about ↑ ((1.2)) I forgot one bear

109 S: *taan*

110 G: what about

111 S: deer↑

112 G: deer↑

113 S: *gaat*

114 G: rat↑

115 S: *kugan*

The fact that there are varied responses, from Haida students and non-Haida students, reveals that here they sense a freedom to participate rather than compete (in accordance with item 13) since the competitive approach would normally end up in silencing the Haidas (see Browne 1990:30). The students provide the answers since they are comfortable with the way the instructor leads the class and asks questions.

The fifth item concerns learning from repeated and silent observation (Pepper & Henry 1987:57). Repetitions of stories, poems, songs and even vocabulary provide opportunities for all students to learn, though the Native American student preference to observe silently is a dominant trait (Macias 1989:48). In the following excerpt, from Appendix G, the instructor notices that some children are having problems with counting and recognizing numbers one to ten in an earlier activity. Genie then decides to model and count twice before allowing the students to answer (lines 434 to 480). The third time through, she invites the students to join her:

481   ": now wait for me I say it first you repeat after *sgwaansing* (one) {holding
482   ":up one finger}

And she proceeds to count to ten with them echoing her counting.

After the counting, she has the students sing The Itsy Bitsy Spider Song for the second time in the lesson,

509   G: good now let's do the *dup'juu 7ul'juu yang a jing* once more
510   U: [*dup'juu 7ul'juu yang a jing*

She then provides more reinforcement of the song that they had sung earlier, and repeats the motions one by one. Thus, repetition serves as a key factor, in this case as the instructor provides the opportunity for the students to observe her counting and to repeat the song they had sung a few minutes earlier. It is not only the Haidas that benefit from repetition, but it encourages all students together as it ratifies the Haida preference to participate when they are ready to try the task (see Hirst & Slavik 1990; Stairs 1993:87 for more information concerning silent observation).

A final example concerns the possibility for students to learn and observe silently as the instructor teaches the lesson. In the following excerpt, the instructor has implemented a hide and seek activity. She asks the student where a picture is using the Haida noun and the student finds the picture, waits for a question, "what did you find?" or "what do you have?" The student then answers the question, and waits for the second question, "and what is [Haida word]?" The student provides the answer and then he must answer a final question, "and what is [English word] in Haida?" To which the student responds and then sits down. The excerpt here reveals the nature of repetition,

218 G: uhhm ((3.4)) Robin can you find me *tsii kultaxun*↑ (mosquito)

219 RH: {goes up and looks through the pictures}

220 G: what do you have↑

221 RH: *tsii kultaxun* (mosquito)

222 G: *aangaa* (yes) and what is *tsii kultaxun*↑ (mosquito)

223 RH: mosquito

224 G: and how do you say mosquito in Haida↑

225 RH: *tsii kultaxun* (mosquito)

226 G: good bring it to me and go to your seat ((.04)) bring it to me

This particular activity seems popular with all the students, perhaps because the format provides plenty of repetition before they actually participate, thus giving them more confidence when they do engage in the activity.

Items 9, taking more time to respond than non-native students, and 10, remaining silent when reprimanded link closely together. The time the teacher waits for a response, wait time, is normally a half a second to a second before a mainstream teacher would echo the question to the student or ask someone else (see Rowe 1974). Tobin and Capie (1980) find that when the wait extends to three seconds, the students provide more thoughtful answers. Erickson and Mohatt in their study note that the Odawa teacher waits three times longer for an answer than her Euro-Canadian counterpart, imparting an "impression of deliberateness and calm in the classroom" (1986:162). The excerpt here, from appendix F, reveals a fairly long wait time:

127 ": your bottoms ((4.5)) okay Katie can you find *ngaal* (kelp)↑

128 KH: *ngaal*

129 G: *aangaa* and can you tell us what a *ngaal* is↑

130 KH: ((3.2)) kelp

131 G: good girl and how do you say kelp in Haida↑

132 KH: *ngaal*

134 Ss: *ngaal*

The extended wait time ensures that the student can answer when ready and after she does answer, the instructor is quick to ratify her response.

Genie reveals that she is patient when she asks for answers and her wait time is variable, dependent on the student, as seen in this excerpt from Appendix G:

360 G: *gaam* Sonny *giisluu*↑ (how many) {holding up 5 fingers}

361 Sy: {no answer}

362 G: ((8.0)) Ronnie *giisluu*↑ (how many) {looking at him showing 5 fingers}

363 R: uhm ((inaudible)) ((4.4))

364 G: *gam* {shaking her head} ahm Brad *giisluu*↑ {holding up 5 fingers}

365 B: ((4.1)) I don't know

366 G: look up here and try and count

367 B: ((5.5)) *tlayhl* (five)

Genie far exceeds the normal half second to one second wait time, with waits ranging from 4.1 seconds in line 365 to 8.0 seconds in line 362. The extended wait time seems to offer the students the notion that their answer is worth the instructor's wait.

Concerning discipline, Philips notes the preference of the Warm Springs Indian parents to discipline their children away from the attention of others (1983:66), which alleviates the possibility of both the parents and child losing face. The following sequence provides an example of a silent response and an illustration of indirect discipline:

150 G: *gaam* (no) *tsii kultaxun* (mosquito) right here Rory what are we missing↑
151 RH: {sits and stares at the instructor but does not answer}
152 Ss: ((3.2)) {some begin to laugh}
153 G: oh let's not laugh okay uhhm Jaymie

The student does not provide the answer Genie sought even with the lengthy wait time, and some other students start laughing. Her reprimand is not direct, but rather indirect in order to allow the students who are laughing to save face as well as to convey to the others that laughing at a classmate is not acceptable. In fact, most of the Haida instructors' reprimands are general, addressing the class as a whole rather than individuals, as we see in this excerpt from appendix F:

175 G: okay we should be sitting on our bottoms that is about the 5th time I told
176 ": you guys to be sitting on your bottoms
177 Ss: {still boisterous}
178 G: okay quietly or we keep you ((late))
179 ?:   shhh shhh

In this section, the instructor addresses the class in the first person plural, *we*, in line 175, and collectively as *you* in both lines 176 and 178 firmly, yet very generally.

It is only when certain students are not paying attention and disturbing the instructor and other students that the instructor then reprimands them by name. This sequence, from Appendix G, reveals a combination of both general and specific reprimands:

425 G: oh let's have all eyes up here okay quit fidgeting Krysia to the edge of the
426 ": carpet and sit on your bottoms ((1.2)) sit on your bottom

427 S: ((5.5)) I'm squished

428 G: sit on your bottom

429 Ss: {start laughing}

430 G: if you guys would sit at the edge of the carpet then you wouldn't be

431 ": squished sit up Asia

432 S: ((5.2)) hey

433 G: Ronnie ((1.5)) we're waiting for Ronnie Kuba and Rufus

434 Ss: {move to the edge of the carpet}

435 G: *howaa (thank you)* Ronnie ((5.3)) kay now I want all eyes up here listen and

436 ": watch ((2.3)) {holding her ears} okay listen and watch are you all watching↑

437 Ss: yeah

438 G: I don't see everyone's eyes on me

There are five general reprimands in this sequence, lines 425, 426, 430, 436, and 438 and all have a non-specific *you* except the last one, 438, which uses *everyone* instead of *you* or *your*. She specifically mentions Krysia in line 425 for fidgeting, Asia to sit up in line 431, and Ronnie, Kuba, and Rufus to move up to the edge of the carpet in line 433. With the general approach to discipline, the students are not subjected to as much embarrassment as they would be for specific disciplinary actions.

The final two items to consider, reluctance to display knowledge others do not have (item 11) and preference not to be spotlighted (12) are also intertwined. The context of this reluctance stems from the culturally inappropriate expression of knowledge (see Philips 1973:383; Wolcott 1974:414) and, interestingly, there is variation on this item with regards to Haida students. In this sequence (from Appendix F and considered previously for reprimands) the instructor has asked a Haida student for an answer but does not get one:

150 G: *gaam* (no) *tsii kultaxun* (mosquito) right here Rory what're we missing↑

151 RH: {sits and stares at the instructor but does not answer}

152 Ss: ((3.2)) {some begin to laugh}

153 G: oh let's not laugh okay uhhm Jaymie

154   JH: {hands in the air} *hlguun*

155   G: good what's *hlguun*↑

156   JH: skunk cabbage

157   G: and how do you say skunk cabbage in Haida↑

158   Ss: *hlguun*

159   JH: *hlguun*

160   G: *hlguun* good we are missing one more what are we missing Vinny↑

She finally does get an answer, after waiting for a while, from another Haida student. The sequence is interesting in that one Haida student is not responding to the spotlight, and another Haida student is willing to answer the question for him and take the spotlight away from him.

Conclusion

Having defined a Haida lesson as the presence of the Haida instructors in an educational setting and any activity in which they engage the class, it is necessary to analyze the data according to criteria of either a craft focused lesson, or a language focused lesson. The results reveal that the Haida students conform to some of the characteristics most of the time, but also contradict some items as well.

In those areas of nonconformity, I have tried to demonstrate that a combination of the instructor's approach and personality and the type of classroom activity, as well as the student's demeanor and class size, account for some of the differences.

Finally, in this chapter I have mentioned issues regarding the Haida instructors, such as teaching style, wait-time, and classroom management, only peripherally. I will consider such aspects in greater depth in the next chapter in order to explore the Haida instructors' presence and influence in the classroom.

Chapter 6
Issues involved in teaching Haida

Introduction

There are many issues to consider regarding Haida instruction. Aspects such as the influence of English phonology on learning Haida phonology; the viability of Haida beyond the classroom; community efforts at language revitalization; and long term results of Haida instruction, are all issues important to consider. Since my interest focuses on Haida student participation in the classroom, I purposely limit my attention to the issues directly influencing students, instructors, and Haida instruction in the classroom environment. I discuss these issues in terms of crucial, primary, and secondary categories and their impact on the students, Haida instructors, and their classes.

The main issue I discuss in the crucial category is time. In the primary category, I address the Haida instructors' teaching style, the curriculum, and social marginalization. Finally, in the secondary category, I consider teacher status and parental attitudes.

The crucial concern regarding the Haida program is time. The issue of time involves how often students have Haida lessons, and the amount of time that they have actual Haida instruction during their lessons. This issue directly impacts all the others, as I will elaborate more fully in the following sections.

Three of the most important primary issues pertain to the teaching style of the Haida instructors, the curriculum, and marginalization. I consider these three in particular since the instructors' teaching styles affect how they teach Haida; the curriculum affects what they teach; and, marginalization affects both the instructors and the students.

The two following secondary issues are important to the instructors, but their impact on the classroom is not as direct as that of the primary issues. The first issue pertains to status, i.e., being a certified teacher. This matter has the instructors seeking alternative avenues for certification, but they have yet to achieve their goal. Secondly, the issue of parental attitudes (as revealed in a community survey) concerning second language instruction provides insight into the Haida program's impact on the children and the community.

The crucial issue

Time is the most crucial issue concerning the Haida language program. There are three important aspects of time that affect the program, the first two which have a direct impact. The first element is the time allotted for Haida instruction. The second element concerns the actual amount of Haida language instruction during the allotted time. Finally, the third element concerns the loss of fluent Haida speaking elders.

Allotted classroom time

There are usually 42 weeks in the school year. The Haida language program starts a week after the school year begins (as mentioned in chapter 3), and the program finishes two weeks before the school year ends. These differences in start date and end date immediately account for three weeks less of Haida instruction. There are, therefore, approximately 39 weeks of potential instruction. Christmas and Easter also account for four weeks of loss as well because crafts dominate the lessons for two weeks prior to each holiday. Thus, of the 42 weeks of instruction, only 35 weeks remain for Haida language instruction.

The classes, 1st to 7th grade, meet twice a week for 30 minutes a lesson. Thus, at best, the Haida program has a possible total of 35 hours of instruction, given that the lessons are 30 minutes each. After attending the program for seven years, the students might possibly receive a total of 245 hours of Haida language instruction. Steven Greymorning (1997) surmises that the minimal time necessary for fluency in another language is 600 to 700 hours (discussed in detail in the next chapter). The total hours of Haida instruction, 35 hours (for the year) multiplied by 7 (for first through seventh grade) totals 245 hours, are possible hours of instruction not the actual hours of instruction, and fall far short of the minimal 600-700 hours Greymorning suggests.

Actual amount of Haida language instruction

If the Haida instructors in fact taught Haida during the allotted time for lessons, then the numbers of hours would not vary from the previous section. The reality is that for each grade and each lesson, the actual amount of Haida instruction varies. As the transcripts indicate, there are art-focused lessons consisting of drawing, crafts, and ornament making. These lessons are primarily English dominant (though the actual crafts could have Haida language instruction incorporated such as terminology for the crafts, including terms for colors, drawing, coloring, cutting and pasting, etc.), and result in less time for actual Haida language instruction.

My limited data concerning the curriculum allows only speculation concerning how often the instructors teach the Haida language. It is possible to surmise that if every third week the instructors had craft focused lessons, drawing and coloring for example, English would then be dominant. That would diminish the 35 possible hours of instruction to less than 24 hours for the year. If all the rest of the lessons were full of Haida instruction, it would only account for 60% percent of potential time, including the time devoted to holiday crafts. Thus, at best, at the end of their 7th year, the students would have a total 147 hours of Haida instruction if the total instruction time were 60 percent of the possible Haida instruction time.

The loss of fluent Haida speaking elders

The last issue concerning time that affects the Haida language program has to do with fluent Haida speaking elders. They range in age from 60 to 90 years and each year the number of elders decreases due to death. With the school's open door policy (the elders are always welcome in the classroom), the Haida language program ultimately suffers as fewer fluent elders can visit the classrooms and participate in the Haida language program. The harsh reality is that soon there will be no more fluent Haida speaking elders as their numbers diminish yearly due to death.

Primary issues

The Haida instructors' teaching style

Classroom management also has important implications for participation. Unfortunately, First Nations and American Indian teaching styles have received little commentary and research. Celia Haig-Brown's experience provides a basis for establishing a distinct native style of teaching (1994). Haig-Brown mentions that she had often heard of a Native teaching style but had not been able to observe this until her graduate studies. In her opening comments, she offers this qualification:

> The experience was an eye-opener for someone who had heard and read about "Native learning and teaching styles" with some skepticism. Although I still argue that the teaching approaches I experienced are not limited to First Nations teachers, and that the First Nations people are not genetically determined to teach in a particular way, I had never before experienced this kind of teaching. It exemplified much of what I had seen attributed to a 'Native teaching style' and was compatible with a 'Native learning style.' (1994:165)

Haig-Brown later explains that the class provided her with experiences that she "had heard talked about as a Native teaching style--a style that closely approximated the traditional way of teaching" (1994:167-8). The comment qualifies the previous statement that she had heard and read about the differences in Native teaching style because there is little research published on this subject.

Her involvement in a beadwork course served as the basis for her observations. Haig-Brown admits that the Native teacher and her teaching approach affected her greatly so that instead of being both a student and an observer, Haig-Brown was wooed by the teacher into being an avid student to the point of foregoing her role as an observer (1994:167-8). This non-pressured setting was effective in persuading Haig-Brown to be an active student rather than a detached observer.

In the most relevant article concerning Native American teaching styles, Gerald Mohatt and Frederick Erickson addressed "data on the implicit culture in the classroom" (1986:136). They compared the cultural organization of participation structures of two Northern Ontario first grade classrooms: one class had an Odawa (Algonkian) teacher and and the other class had a Euro-Canadian teacher. They observed that the Indian (their term) teacher avoided explicit evaluation of correctness and usually did not correct student responses explicitly nor did she praise them explicitly (1986:160). In contrast, the Haida instructors Genie and Dora practiced both explicit correction and explicit praise, as I discuss further when analyzing the transcripts.

Other observations Erickson and Mohatt noted were differences in the form of address and directives. The Odawa teacher used fewer directives to individual "auditors" in all three categories of questions, imperatives, and nonimperative statements. She also used more directives in the form of questions directed at a general audience, but fewer in the imperative and statement. Overall, the Odawa teacher gave far fewer directives in the other two categories: 7 imperatives compared to 36 by the Euro-Canadian and 7 statements compared to 24 by the Euro-Canadian (1986:153). This chapter will contrast the Haida instructors' use of directives because of their style and the nature of their language instruction. At times the Haida instructors employed general directives, allowing anyone to respond. At other times they specifically directed queries or comments to students.

Erickson and Mohatt noted other variables concerning class control. There were differences in overt control of the class. The Odawa teacher had a closer relationship, physically, to the students in that the directives that were specific were also in close proximity, usually face-to-face, to the student rather than across the classroom. The Euro-Canadian differed in his calling across the room to specific students, and his proxemic relationship was also more spatially distant (1986:151).

Lastly, there were significant differences in time spent on classroom activities. The Odawa allowed more time for the students to enter the class and settle. In over 7 instances her class took 43.7 minutes to enter and settle, approximately six minutes per class. Her Euro-Canadian counterpart's class took 28.7 minutes, or approximately 4 minutes per class to settle. She took 5.3 minutes to distribute paper during two instances compared to 1.2 minutes in the Euro-Canadian's class for the same number of instances. She had more instances of circulating to give individual attention, 11, for a total of 225 minutes, averaging approximately 20.45 minutes with each student. Her counterpart had only 6 instances for a total of 177.5 minutes, but averaged 29.5 minutes with each student. Thus, the Euro-Canadian actually spent more time with individual students, though the Odawa teacher spent time with more students.

In small group work, both teachers gave approximately 10 percent of their time to individual attention while sitting. The difference was that the Odawa teacher had more instances (4), for a total of 58.7 minutes and her counterpart had only one instance that took 50.2 minutes.

Three situations are significant regarding their differences: small group work, waiting for the class, and free time to play in class. The Odawa teacher had 3 instances of waiting which totaled 66.6 minutes whereas her counterpart had 1 occasion and took 15.8 minutes. A major difference was the time in waiting for the class to settle down and pay attention to the teacher. The Odawa teacher spent 36.2 minutes waiting for the class during 4 instances. The Euro-Canadian had no instances of waiting for his class. Finally, concerning free time to play, there were no instances of such activity in the Odawa class and 2 instances in the Euro-Canadian class accounting for a total of 26.3 minutes (Erickson & Mohatt 1986:144).

In one more related article, Lynne McAlpine, Alice Eriks-Brophy, and Martha Crago (1996) addressed teaching beliefs in Mohawk classrooms. They considered the influence of "personal history, sociocultural history and teaching beliefs surrounding language and culture" in order to assess the "ways in which cultural identity and language impact on these beliefs" (1996:390). They compared three teachers, two Mohawk women and one "nonaboriginal" mainstream woman with Japanese background, concerning how teacher beliefs affected performance in the classroom. The writers presented the research as a study of contrasts, even between the two Mohawk teachers though they were from the same community. Although born and raised in the same community, one of the Mohawk teachers did not learn to speak Mohawk. The other teacher learned Mohawk as a child, but as she grew older, she spoke more English until she started doing substitute teaching, after which she began speaking (and eventually teaching) Mohawk on a daily basis.

As part of the research each teacher worked closely with the authors to produce a concept map. The Mohawk speaking teacher had five modules linked to teaching, the central module: listening, respect, sharing, language (aboriginal), and culture (McAlpine, Brophy, & Crago 1996:398). The Mohawk teacher who could not speak her language had six modules connected to teaching: culture, family, listening, tension, being distinct, and language (aboriginal). The mainstream teacher also had six modules connected to teaching: administrative support, culture, discrete, (whole) language, listening/sharing, and changes in practice (McAlpine, Brophy, & Crago 1996:403). There are lines connecting her modules explaining the relationship of the modules, for example culture (is) discrete (from) teaching.

There were three areas of similarities in the teachers' mapping. First, all three had listening as an important module concerning teaching. They all also had language modules, but the mainstream teacher's interest was whole language as a teaching approach (see Reyhner and Rickey [1991] for a discussion about whole language in Native American education). The Mohawk teachers also had a language module, but the difference was the importance of the aboriginal language (Mohawk) in their daily life. The Mohawk who taught her language did not see language as a problem, but the Mohawk teacher who taught in English saw the language issue as problematic because of her lack of skills in Mohawk and its implications for greater cultural identity. Finally, all three had culture as important modules, but the difference was that the Mohawk-speaking teacher did not limit that module to Mohawk culture only, while the other two teachers did.

I want to discuss Native American teaching styles in order to assess the influence of instructors' style on the students' participation. Along with Erickson and Mohatt's claim of implicit cultural influences on teaching style (1986:136), I suggest that the Haida instructors' style greatly impacts both student participation and their approach to classroom management. The Haida instructors have four distinct differences in teaching that influence their teaching performance. These areas are: a) expectation of participation differences; b) participation requirements; c) proxemic differences; and d) classroom management styles.

First Nations teachers seem to blend historical learning with the current classroom learning environment. That Native Americans have a distinct teaching style, which however has received little academic attention, seems to indicate that it is subtle and non-imposing.

Beginning with expectations in participation, Haig-Brown considered her own beading class experience and explained "I don't really like the colours, but I don't expect to do much anyway. I was planning just to take notes...Both teachers and students clearly assume I will participate" (1994:166). As she attended more sessions, she was not able to "just take notes." The instructor had wooed Haig-Brown in to fully participating.

This aspect of wooing the students into participating fits with the Haida instructors' relaxed notion of expected participation. It is also controversial, or unusual at the very least since in most other teachers' philosophy or approach, the participatory process is obligatory. That is, mainstream teachers often see the classroom setting as a place for students not only to gain knowledge but to display it as well (Philips 1972a&b; 1983). As the sole authority in the classroom, mainstream teachers require students to participate regardless of the students' desire or preference. The Haida instructors, on the other hand, allow greater student autonomy in participation. This student autonomy, a strong cultural value, is consistent with situated learning (Lave and Wenger 1991:51), of learning within a relevant cultural manner and within one's community (Kleinfield 1972).

In the context of learning within a particular community and within a specific setting, the Haida instructors encourage legitimate peripheral participation. Their teaching style is not ineffective nor pressured for participation, but is socio-culturally sensitive (Lave & Wenger 1991:52). When First Nations students are in such an environment, their willingness to participate increases with their confidence in the subject. Also, when they know that they can contribute to the classroom at their discretion, it fosters a greater willingness to participate.

For Lave and Wenger, the learning process brings students from the periphery as learners or observers where they acquire knowledge and/or skills necessary to be a member in their community, and to the forefront as experts once they have mastered the subject (1991:56). Applying Lave and Wenger's participatory notion to the Haida instructors, it is most revealing that autonomy is both important and respected. In situations where native students are forced to participate, the typical response is silence or even a wrong answer because of prematurely bringing them to the center of the participatory process. They are forced to be skillful or manifest knowledge beyond their community standards and norms (Philips 1972a:182). In such situations, the native student, within the context of the regular classroom, participates in such a way that forces the teacher to ask someone else for the correct answer. This becomes strategic behavior because the student knows that being silent, just shrugging his shoulders (see Feyereisen & de Lannoy [1991] for more about gestures and language), or giving the wrong answer redirects the teacher's attention to someone else (see Plank 1994:10). The Haida instructors' style of teaching reduces this stress and promotes greater freedom in the classroom.

The relaxed expectations for participation have a direct influence on the teachers' demands for participation. Even in the Haida language program, where participation is crucial, the instructors' demand is modified to reduce the stress factor and allow the students greater concentration on the language. The instructors have created an environment that lowers anxiety in what Krashen (1982) describes as the affective filter, a socio-psychological factor that influences one's ability to learn languages. It is a filter that allows or prevents language acquisition based on various socio-affective factors, most importantly the learners' level of anxiety. The optimal language learning condition is one that maintains the affective filter with low anxiety levels, and the Haida instructors seem to maintain such a level in their lessons.

Concerning proxemics, differences abound when comparing teaching styles. The current standard distance from the students is full of legal concerns which, for the sake of safety, requires minimal contact and therefore, imposed distancing. As a result, the attitude, based on fear of legal reprisal, is to refrain from actual contact as much as possible, and when contact is necessary, to do so in the most inoffensive manner possible. My own observations reveal the Haida instructors are approaching students on a personal level, that teaching Haida does not require formal distance. Rather, the instructors see learning Haida as an important extension of their daily experience.

To exemplify my point, I have chosen an incident that captures the instructors' approach. A Haida student had mentioned to the mainstream teacher that she was having pain. The mainstream teacher then informed both Haida instructors. Dora, after hearing the information, walked over to the student to ask about her condition. The instructor had gently caressed her head and shoulder as she asked the question. She stopped and leaned on the student's desk. She was eye level with the student as she held the student's hand and listened to her problem. Such instances were not uncommon, and are indicative of the instructors' preference for contact.

Two important classroom management issues include different noise level tolerance and freedom of student movement. The mainstream teachers have low tolerance of noise, in contrast to the Haida instructors who allow a greater amount of noise before commenting or implementing authority. That is, the mainstream teachers are quick to stifle any activity unrelated to the lesson at hand (see Erickson and Mohatt 1986:144; McAlpine & Taylor 1993). They do not allow students to converse with one another over their instruction, in keeping with the notion that the sole authority, the teacher, decides who and when anyone other than him or herself can speak (see Philips 1972a:170).

In contrast, the Haida instructors have a much greater tolerance of noise and interruptions. In fact, the students seem to be free to wander or speak at any time they so desire. One instance of noise level occurred when the class was supposed to be working on their Christmas ornaments. Most of the students were either standing or visiting with another student. At this point, Genie reproached the students for their loudness. The level of noise was not as bad as it had been at other times during the lesson, but Genie decided it was unacceptable, as the transcript reveals:

S: {getting very loud}

G: oh oh oh we're getting too loud {walks to the back of the class} ((3.0))

The class did quiet down temporarily. It was nearly the end of the lesson, they were ready to quit, and the noise remained at a constant level, though not enough to disturb the Haida instructors.

It is important to note that this instance represents a particular lesson which was not language based, i.e., there was no Haida instruction. Rather, it was a Christmas decoration making lesson with Haida themes. Since they were making Haida Christmas tree ornaments and other things, when they were finished, or bored, the students had greater freedom to roam and visit other students than they would have had during a lesson focusing on Haida language instruction. What is also important is that the Haida instructors exercise more tactile contact with their students as well as allowing them greater freedom to speak and roam in the classroom during lessons that are not language-instruction based.

One final example which reveals the Haida instructors' approach concerns how students refer to the instructors. In the classes I observed, the students maintained a strict distance from the mainstream teachers using the appropriate Mr. or Ms. title followed by their last name. While in their office, I asked the Haida instructors about this and their response reveals their attitude:

F: do you have a problem with the students calling you Mrs. Dora, or Dora↑

D: They call me

F: auntie

D: Dora some call me *nana* and some call me auntie the little Kindergartens

": want to call me *nana*, that's okay...that's all right

F: Dora ((0.6)) and Genie calls them friends

D: yeah little friends

T: My daughter loves Genie

D: oh she's such a good teacher she is so good with them kids

T: Rory use to call her auntie Genie when he used to come home from

": Kindergarten he used to say oh my aunt Genie

F: really↑

D: Rory Ethan still calls her auntie Genie

F: really

D: yeah

Both Dora and Genie prefer the informal approach as indicated in this section of the transcript. Dora, the eldest of the two instructors, mentions her approval of being called *nana* (grandma), as well as auntie, which offers a sense of family. In some cases the term *nana* may actually be appropriate because of her biological relationship to the student, but for most students, it is a term of endearment and not a kinship relationship since even the Euro-Canadian children refer to Dora and Genie in these terms.

Finally, to end with two unsolicited confirmations, a mainstream teacher, who happened to be using the laminator as I asked this question, added her own son and daughter's experience attesting to the students' bond with the Haida instructors. Her comments, "She loves Genie" and "He still calls her auntie" revealed the level of intimacy the instructors had with their students. This affinity was even further manifested as we left the 7th grade class after the lesson and came upon a Euro-Canadian female student entering the classroom. She saw us coming out of the class and warmly greeted the Haida instructor by her first name. Then, reflectively, she immediately commented that of all the teachers she had had or currently had, only the Haida instructors allowed students to address them by their first names and she appreciated them for that.

The Haida curriculum

As mentioned in Chapter 2, there are many issues that arise when the word "curriculum" is mentioned. There are three particular issues worth addressing concerning the Haida curriculum: 1. the lack of an official Haida curriculum; 2. the content of the unofficial curriculum; and 3. the use of songs in the unofficial curriculum.

Haida curriculum development has had two phases: the first was K-7 and was developed in 1994, and then a newer updated version appeared beginning in 1996. Largely due to a governmental education grant, a search for a curriculum developer in 1993 secured the development of the first curriculum, completed in May, 1994. The latter is the effort of the Haida Gwaii First Nations Education

Coordinator, whose position began after the completion of the first curriculum, largely due to educational grants received to develop the curriculum to the 12th grade.

When asked if they were using the most recent curriculum, the instructors responded negatively and explained their frustration with its style and content. The curriculum issue (or lack of an official curriculum) is one that adversely affects the program since there is no clear systematic approach used in the Haida program. Although there are two completed curricula, the instructors refuse to use the current one citing the problems aforementioned and while they like the first curriculum, they do not use it. Thus, what they utilize during their lessons is vocabulary based, though not necessarily from an official curriculum; they teach mainly vocabulary items.

The curriculum content, what is actually taught, is also of importance. There are two main approaches involving language revitalization: the first concerns a language and culture approach in which the Native American language is part of a cultural curriculum (see Leap 1988 for a discussion concerning American Indian language renewal issues). In this approach, the main goal is not necessarily fluency, but a general knowledge of culture with sprinklings of vocabulary and phrases (see Palmer 1988:308). The second approach is fluency based. The content and approach are specifically designed and taught with the goal of producing fluent speakers (Greymorning 1997). Most such approaches are immersion-based and require diligence from both teachers and students.

The Haida Language program on Haida Gwaii resembles that of a language and culture approach with a strong vocabulary emphasis. With only an hour a week of instruction (at the most), the students have less than 40 hours of Haida instruction per year, not nearly enough for them to venture beyond the lexical level of usage in class and outside the classroom.

I queried the instructors' perception of obstacles in teaching Haida. Without having the guidance of an official curriculum, in this sequence, the instructors discuss one of their difficulties:

F: so what has been the most difficult thing to teach about Haida↑

G: the language

E: ((loud laughter))

D: Genie has been a real good student she learns good

F: uhmm hmm

G: not having the resources

D: yeah

G: you know because kids are so used of text books

F: oh yeah

G: and that's something we don't have but next year we'll have it I'm going

":   to develop it somehow

This sequence reveals their concerns about the lack of resources. They both agreed that the students would be more involved if they had actual textbooks that they could see as being specifically for Haida language instruction.

I had initially thought Haida orthography would have been an important issue, but it was not. The instructors have accepted and adopted a modified orthographic version doubling vowels to distinguish vowel length. The instructors have incorporated some of the recent research John Enrico has done as he collected data for a new Haida dictionary he has compiled (Enrico 2005).

Finally, I want to address the use of songs in the curriculum. The inclusion of Haida songs in the lessons has been very effective, whether it was body parts, as in "Head and shoulders" or adaptations of the "Itsy bitsy spider," children were eager to sing and do the motions for the songs. What is notable is that both the songs are adaptations of English songs with their rhythms and stresses. Haida words, grafted into the melody without regard to Haida inflection or rhythm, appear in the songs and ultimately are subjected to English rhythm and stress patterns, such as the Haida version of "Ten little Indians" or "Head and shoulders, knees and toes." Traditional Haida singing is not part of the lessons, though with the students' enjoyment of singing and vocabulary acquisition, it seems that the instructors might profitably include some traditional or even contemporary Haida songs in the lessons.

Marginalization

The difficulties already mentioned make teaching Haida arduous, but it is necessary to add one more element concerning the instructor's efforts, that of marginalization. According to the *American Heritage College Dictionary*, the definition of marginalize is "to relegate or confine to a lower or outer limit or edge, as of social standing" (1993:829). Thus, it must be inferred that marginalization can be both spatial and social. For the Haida instructors, marginalization, being spatially and socially on the periphery or the sidelines, occurs on a daily basis. They endure marginalization in three settings: 1. in their office; 2. in the classrooms; and 3. in their professional capacity.

The first arena of marginalization for the Haida instructors begins in their office. The school is U shaped with the main hall as the entrance and a few trailers serving as extra classrooms. The Haida instructors' office is located at the northern end of the adjacent hallway (the second bar of the "U") and next to the exit. The instructors do not necessarily see this location as marginal, but the fact that it is located away from all the other offices, which are at the front of the school, suggests that this location originally served some other function, such as a janitor's closet. It is a small office with only enough room for a couple of chairs, a small wall table, a mid-sized table and some shelves for the Haida language material. There is a phone, a coffee machine, and a laminator, a machine that wraps paper items with heated plastic and then forms a protective covering as it cools. At one time, there was an old MacIntosh 512, but someone took it away.

During the time that I was there observing, a few students visited for social reasons not necessarily having to do with Haida language. One teenager stopped by specifically to say thank you for use of a drum and for clarification of a Haida song he was learning. As for the staff and faculty, most of them visit in order to use the laminator, the only one in the school (and, apparently, with no other possible location for it). If the laminator were not in the Haida instructors' room, the traffic would be limited only to those interested in speaking with the instructors.

Marginalization encountered in the classroom falls into two different categories. The first is most often in the form of outside interruption (i.e., someone coming into the classroom even though they are not part of the class), which happens almost routinely. These interruptions are, for the most part, someone that the instructors know who is in the class vicinity when they see the Haida instructors and decide to visit. The second type occurs within the classroom, from the mainstream teachers and their aides.

The first type of interruption happens when people, most of them not part of the class being taught, suddenly decide to drop in and visit the class. It may seem as though this is simply an interruption, but when considering the prospect of doing the same to any class other than the Haida language class, it is marginalization since it is not possible to visit other classes. There is no similar freedom to interrupt mainstream classes in order to visit with the teacher or students. This exclusivity for visitation marginalizes the instructors and their lessons.

The other type of marginalization within the classroom comes from both mainstream teachers and their TA's. Since the Haida instructors go from classroom to classroom to teach, very often the mainstream teacher remains present in the classroom. The Haida instructors mentioned that occasionally the mainstream teachers participate in the lesson as well, but I never observed such a situation. What I have observed is mainstream teachers staying behind to prepare for the next lesson. Since they are the mainstream teachers, and it is their classroom, the Haida instructors have the attention of the students only temporarily. The mainstream teachers often discuss things with their TA to the point that it is distracting to the lesson, though they are oblivious to that fact.

If these were isolated incidents, I would not find it necessary to comment, but the following transcript excerpt (see Appendix C for full transcript), exemplifies how the mainstream teacher and TA's conversations override the classroom. In this example, the students were making some Christmas ornaments when the mainstream teacher returned to the classroom. She was preparing activities for the class after the Haida lesson was over and then the TA approach her off camera at her desk.

136 G: SHHHHH
137 MT: put it back on these
138 S: look
139 G: oh let's not put our shoes on the table
140 MT: and if not if there's ((unclear))
141 G: remember we need to stay in our own spot in our space
142 TA: they due today↑
143 MT: yes
144 TA: okay so do what could I do here and then just keep that one in my box
145 G: Pam did you start already↑
146 P: what↑
147 A: just put it in your box
148 G: oh no Pam Asia
149 TA: OK
150 MT: see you later
151 TA: okay

This section of transcript begins with the Haida instructor telling the class to be quiet. As was the case throughout the class, the mainstream teacher (MT) and her teacher assistant (TA) are discussing things for later that day. In the 16 lines of this excerpt, they have 9 of the lines, well over half of the turns in this section. What is most interesting is that they are conversing without any regard to the class. In fact, because the Haida instructor had told the class to be quiet, the conversation between the mainstream teacher and her TA stands out even more. In all fairness, during this sequence the students were working on Christmas ornaments, and their actual language instruction was over. Nevertheless, during my observations, whether the students are engaged in Haida instruction or other "Haida activities," the mainstream teachers often used that time to plan for lessons and invariably talked throughout and over the lesson.

Whether the instructors see competition with mainstream teachers' lesson planning as marginalization or just part of their work environment is difficult to say. The instructors are grateful for the opportunity to be in the classrooms to teach Haida. But the question of validity concerning both the importance of Haida and the Haida instructors most likely arises in the students' minds as they constantly hear their mainstream teacher discussing lesson plans over the Haida instruction and are aware that the mainstream teachers would never allow such discussion if they were trying to teach. It conveys to the students that Haida is unimportant, resulting in symbolic domination of English and intellectual devaluation of Haida. It seems that the Haida classroom environment has yet to experience that "in order for First Nations language and culture to survive and flourish, equality with official languages is crucial (Report of the Assembly of First Nations language and literacy secretariat 1992:47).

Secondary Issues

Status and certification

A significant concern of the Haida instructors is that of being approved or certified for full teacher status rather than just being instructors. They have taken a couple of introductory linguistics courses, acted as consultants for the curriculum being developed, and attended teaching methodology sessions, but since they do not have college degrees, their chances for actual promotion to certified teacher status is limited.

They continue to teach Haida without the certification. This has economic consequences (a lower payscale). Administratively, the issue encompasses multileveled concerns that include pay, benefits, and qualifications, all of which would be achieved once they attained their teacher status. It is an important issue, not just for the Haida instructors, but for any instructor not certified as a teacher.

Parental attitudes

A 1993 survey of students and parents for Haida Gwaii school district provides insightful information concerning school in general and about the language programs. Unfortunately, the survey only included percentages and not the number of respondents in the survey, though the information extracted from the percentages appears valuable enough to include here.

Since the Haida program is relatively recent (both instructors have been teaching for eight years), parental attitudes provide insight to the community acceptance of the program. Within the backdrop of restricted language use as a result of residential schools, parents that endured hostility towards First Nations languages as they went to school are now in a position to see the reverse of their experiences, that of seeing native language promotion and use in school. Vivian Ayoungman suggests that opportunities to learn a First Nations language are empowering to the students and, in his discussion concerning parental reluctance, he notes that often parents thought that the Native language would negatively affect their children's English abilities (1995:183). For some parents, the issue is difficult because it stirs painful memories, but the general attitude seems to be cautiously favorable.

The survey had 35 questions with three options for response: satisfied, dissatisfied, and undecided. The results of the first question reveal 78% of the parents being satisfied with what their children were learning, 14% dissatisfied, and 9% undecided. It is curious, therefore, that the penultimate question, "degree to which your school has prepared your child for the next level of education," had 57% satisfied, 21 percent dissatisfied, and 23% undecided. Concerning specific subject, 68% indicated their satisfaction with the language programs while 20% percent were dissatisfied and 12% undecided. It is unfortunate that the target languages, Haida and French, are not queried separately since this would reflect the community's response more accurately.

Currently, parental attitudes only minimally impact the Haida language program. Should the community decide to make Haida instruction a priority within the curriculum and demand more time for lessons--a right they have according to the governmental rulings--they could easily change their current secondary position in terms of importance to primary or even crucial level.

Conclusion

The crucial issue in the Haida language program that must be addressed is time. The number of hours of actual Haida instruction per year amounts to less than 24 hours per year. With the program as it is, there are less than 168 hours of Haida instruction from Kindergarten through seventh grade. There needs to be more than just two weekly lessons and within those lessons, more actual Haida language instruction.

Of the primary issues I have dealt with, curriculum and marginalization affect the program adversely and need attention in order to accomplish the goal of producing Haida speakers. Though curriculum development and implementation are more easily addressed (since the instructors can adopt either of the previously developed curricula), the issue of marginalization remains more difficult due to at least these two factors: the general lack of respect for the instructors during their instruction; and the limiting factor of the instructors' status.

Finally, greater parental interest and demand could persuade the administration to increase the quantity and quality of their children's Haida lessons. They could challenge both the administration, which occasionally welcomes more Haida community involvement, and the instructors to adopt a curriculum for each grade which would impact the Haida language instruction beyond a collection of seemingly unrelated vocabulary words, and thereby influence actual fluency beyond the confines of the school's classrooms. The instructors and parents should seek more time for the Haida lessons insisting that on a gradual basis, the goal for the Haida program for each grade must increase the number of lessons and their duration. Concerning the earlier years, Kindergarten through 5th, the parents could seek greater community involvement from the elders and request to have the Haida program meet three times a week for an hour each time. Since the school voices support for greater cultural implementation, increasing the amount of lessons per week as well increasing lesson length is crucial for consistency and greater contact with the language. This change would increase the Haida language program's potential hours of instruction by 105 hours a year, totaling 525 hours by the time the students enter the sixth grade.

The teachers and parents should also insist on the students' having daily hour-long lessons in their 6th and 7th years. This is the crucial period for students to put into practice their Haida language ability from once every second day, to a daily experience, at the very least, in the classroom. These two years alone, with the increased lesson time on a daily basis, would have a total of 350 hours of Haida lessons.

At the very least, the Haida language program must begin by fully utilizing the time currently allotted for Haida language instruction. With parental pressure and administrative approval, the program could expand the length of the lessons as well as the frequency of lessons per week. With the implementation of an accepted curriculum for each grade, the teachers could then foster a greater appreciation for the language by eliminating English as much as possible from the beginning of the program and by teaching communicative competence (appropriate grammatical and socio-cultural language skills) in Haida.

Chapter 7

Conclusion

Currently there are many Native American Language Programs in both Canada and the United States. Kate Freeman, Arlene Stairs, Evelyn Corbiere & Dorothy Lazore (1995) discuss the Ojibwe, Mohawk, and Inuktitut in Canada; Andersen (2000) discusses the Klallam in Washington; Peterson (1997) discusses the Navajo in Arizona; and Wolfson (2000) discusses the Paiute in Utah; these four programs are just a few of the many examples of language revitalization efforts in North America. Of the vast field, I have chosen to review one instance of a language renewal effort as a comparison to my research: The Arapaho in Wisconsin.

One important goal appears within the Arapaho language program that is similar to the Haida language program, that of fluency. The Haida and Arapaho are similar in number, almost 6,000 members, and Arapaho children have not been learning Arapaho as a first language for the last 40 years (Greymorning 1997:23), just as the Haida have not for nearly the same amount of time. According to Celce-Murcia and Larsen-Freeman (1983:524) important aspects of communicative competence, as pertaining to fluency in a language, include not only grammatical knowledge and ability, but important socio-cultural aspects of language as well, such as knowing how to respectfully disagree, how to persuade, how to use correct forms of negation, or how turn-taking and pacing occur in the language. The differences in the Arapaho teaching experience and program goal achievements offer beneficial insight to the Haida language program in regard to the challenge of producing fluent Haida speakers.

Steve Greymorning (1997), motivated by information he had seen on Hawaiian immersion results, wanted to try an immersion approach with the Arapaho. First, assessing the 15 minute daily Arapaho lessons the Kindergarten students were having, he surmised that during the year, the students had approximately 45 hours of instruction. His first pilot, from January to May 1993, implemented hour long immersion lessons with fifteen students from three regular classes (control classes), taking five students from each class.

The students had fifteen sessions at three different language stations, and each station had a different teacher. At the end of their language station lessons, a fourth teacher came to the lesson and then asked them to respond to commands or do various tasks. Greymorning notes:

> After twelve weeks had elapsed, 80% of the test class had mastered 162 words and phrases. This included a list of 32 phrases such as *stand up, sit down, come here, are you hungry, yes I am hungry, what are you doing, I am jumping, what is your name, my name is, write your name, are you thirsty, I am thirsty, pick it up, throw it away, put it down, come in, throw it* (for both animate and inanimate objects), *go and get it, give it to me.* (1997:26)

In comparing these students' progress to the control classes, Greymorning notes the students in the three control classes had mastered between 15 and 18 words by the end of that school year.

Greymorning had considered the Hawaiian immersion data and noted that fluency began after between 600 and 700 contact hours of exposure (1997:27). With only 15 minute daily lessons, he calculated that it would take over 13 years of instruction to achieve the minimum contact hours needed for fluency. He slowly implemented changes at the Kindergarten level and eventually secured half of the school day for the children to learn Arapaho. From the previous 45 hours of instruction per year, the Kindergarten students had approximately 540 contact hours. Noting that with 60 to 160 hours there was a lack in developing fluency, Greymorning remarked that even at the end of the 1995 school year, the students were not fluent. Although the students could maintain conversations in the classroom in Arapaho, and the lessons exceeded more than 90% Arapaho, Greymorning noted that the students were still not on the threshold of fluency.

For Greymorning, the goal of fluency in Arapaho is essential. He mentions that the lexical approach is limited because it does not promote fluency. This approach is a vocabulary based curriculum emphasizing memorization of lexical items from different word classes such as nouns, verbs, and adjectives but does not promote the ability to formulate basic sentences, though it is possible to produce phrases in combination with the vocabulary (see Lewis 1997 for a discussion of implementing the lexical approach). Greymorning suggests it is necessary to challenge the lexical approach and its limitations. He explains when "a speaker possesses the ability to go beyond saying isolated words and phrases," the ability to formulate or manipulate the language effectively with little hesitation, then "they are recognized as fluent" (1997:26).

The Arapaho language renewal efforts provide encouragement for the Haida efforts. Considering the similar circumstances in allotted Haida lesson time, the goal of fluency is impossible with only 35 hours of instruction a year. But within the time that the Haida instructors have, it is possible to go beyond the lexical level of instruction and offer communicative opportunities for the students to use more than numbers, colors, and nouns in isolated responses.

There are many difficulties to consider in language revitalization efforts. For issues related specifically to the Haida, those I observed in the classroom include:

1.   Curriculum development and implementation: That there are two developed curricula with neither one implemented is detrimental to the purpose of the Haida Language Program. Implementing a curriculum for all the grade levels would assist the Haida instructors with consistent lesson content and a greater possibility of building on prior knowledge from grade to grade.

2. Teaching problematic aspects of grammar and phonology: Both of these are not peculiar to any foreign language class since both the phonology and grammar of second language instruction require intentional focus. The phonemic inventory of Haida may be difficult initially for the students, but with attention to the prior issue, this would be much more controllable. It is important to go beyond teaching only at the lexical level with no focus on fluency or communicative competence: vocabulary is important, but the ability to understand and produce utterances at the sentential and discourse level is a key for language renewal. Thus, explicit instruction on Haida grammar seems appropriate. The task of teaching the grammar involves greater preparation for the instructors, but with the communicative approach, the potential result is greater usage of the Haida language.

3. Resources in a consistent orthography: This issue remains problematic since it would be an immense undertaking to find all the research done on Haida grammar and phonology and standardize the orthography (such task requires a specialist that could gather and standardize the historical texts, thus making it more accessible to the teachers and even the rest of the tribe). At the very least, having the instructors develop their own materials is a possibility and a desire of some instructors but time and money prevent this from actually happening.

4. Not making the local school bear the burden for renewing the language: Since most native speakers are not teachers, removing the burden from the school as well as using the language beyond the school would address this issue. Joshua Fishman states that it requires community effort, dedication, and time to reverse language shift and that efforts should be not focused only at the school level (Fishman 1991:368).

5. English in the Haida lessons: This is an issue that fluctuates depending on the content of the lesson. I have observed Haida lessons containing degrees of English ranging from mostly English to very little English. The content should dictate what level is best. But in actual Haida instruction, as opposed to Haida crafts and drawing (though these could also be entirely in Haida), the least amount

of English certainly is best because it permits more exposure to and usage of Haida.

6. Respect from the mainstream teachers: This issue needs some clarification since I suspect mainstream teachers do have some level of respect for the Haida instructors. What is necessary is a greater demonstration of that respect during Haida lessons by participating with the class or by being respectfully quiet.

7. Marginalization: In relation the previous issue, the mainstream teachers' attitude and demeanor can effectively eliminate this from the classroom by respecting the instructors' time in the classroom. The mainstream teachers can instill negative impressions in students when they maintain conversations or discussions with their teaching assistants during the Haida lessons. With more esteem for the Haida instructors and their lessons, marginalization in the classroom need not be an issue in the future.

Currently, the state of ancestral languages among Native American tribes reflects various conditions for the languages. The Diné (Navajo) have over 130,000 native speakers of their language with some children learning it as a first language (Lyovin 1997:312). Even so, there is a concern because some children learn to speak English first and some elders feel their language is now endangered as well. Other tribes, such as the Haida, are not able to boast such numbers. Thus, when even the Diné, who have such numbers, are concerned about losing their language, how much more should the Haida be disquieted!

Fear of language loss is a global issue since throughout the world, many cultures currently struggle with losing their language (Grenoble and Whaley 1998:viii; Hale 1998). Motivated by this fear, there is a growing concern among both Native Americans and scholars to implement efforts at preserving Native American languages (for a discussion of such efforts for Tlingit, Haida, and Tsimshian in Southeastern Alaska, see Dauenhauer and Dauenhauer [1998]; see Jacobs [1998] concerning issues of Mohawk language instruction). Much research has confirmed the positive aspects of language renewal efforts in North America: Brandt (1988:235) suggests that using the ancestral language improves academic performance. Cummins (1991:786) strongly favors bilingual education in the minority language and considers such education as a method for empowering students for success (1986). Kroskrity suggests "rethinking some of the norms of educational policy and practice" (1986:99) in order to improve the educational situation of Native Americans. He suggests "research along such lines will provide Native American communities both with a means of controlling their linguistic resources and with a basis for appropriate educational reforms" (1988:109). Eastman (1979b), Hayes (1990), and Leap (1988) also confirm that local community involvement concerning Native American languages and educational matters is crucial.

Present research points to an undeniable conclusion that maintaining the ancestral language is extremely important. With much of the current language renewal effort relegated to the local schools, understanding different participation styles of Native American students provides insight and implications for ancestral language pedagogy.

Native American participation styles have been the subject of much research. I have considered how Haida participation in the classroom is similar to observations made by Crago (1992), Dumont (1972), John (1972), Macias (1989), Philips (1972a, 1983), Swisher (1990), Swisher and Deyhle (1989), and Wauters et.al. (1989) and that such participation on the part of the Haidas is unlike that of their Euro-Canadian classmates' style.

My observations concerning the distinct participation style among the Haida have particular relevance for learning Haida as a second language. If Haida students do not participate actively in the Haida lessons, then efforts to teach them are in vain. The findings here suggest that the Haida students will participate with adjustments to teaching methodology, specifically, addressing the Haida students' need for a more holistic approach that outlines the goals of the instruction will help to promote the students interaction. With such an approach, the guidelines would include emphasis on a communicative curriculum that highlights group interaction, language that the children use daily and an environment that recognizes the importance of Haida.

Friere suggested that one key to a culture's survival is its language (1985:187-188); therefore, it is important to understand how formal education can promote both language survival as well as language learning when teaching methodologies and curriculum utilize knowledge of different participation styles in the classroom. In one of the earliest policy papers, *Indian Control of Indian Education*, the authors foresaw that,

> Native teachers and counsellors who have an intimate understanding of Indian traditions, psychology, way of life and language are best able to create the learning environment suited to habits and interests of the Indian child. (National Indian Brotherhood 1972:18)

The policy paper also addresses the issue of marginalization as well. Acknowledging the problems one encounters in Native American education, the authors write, "Responsibility for integration belongs to the people involved. It cannot be legislated or promoted without the full consent and participation of the Indians and non-Indians concerned" (National Indian Brotherhood 1972:30). Specifically for the Haida situation, the Haida instructors need greater cooperation from the mainstream teachers during the Haida lessons so that there is no competition for students' attention. If the mainstream teachers cannot participate, they should respect the Haida instructors' need for student attention without creating any competition when they remain in the classroom to discuss lesson plans with their own teaching assistants.

Finally, the situation of the Haida learning their ancestral language as a second language is not uncommon. But what is uncommon, in light of ancestral language curriculum, is the effort to adapt teaching methodology to learning styles in order to foster greater Native American student participation. This book is my contribution specifically to that end.

In sum, the prospect of different participatory styles among the Haida has at least a twofold implication: First, adaptations to teaching methodology are necessary for the students to effectively learn and enthusiastically participate in the Haida Language program; and secondly, the curriculum must reflect relevant language content (beyond the lexical focus) that enhances learning and participation in a manner inclusive of different learning and participation styles.

Finally, there are two issues that greatly affect Haida language revitalization efforts. The first issue concerns western linguistic ideology and the second concerns how that ideology influences pedagogical efforts. Consistently seen within Western (Western European) language ideologies is the propensity to esteem the dominant language ideologies over the minority languages. This is natural, according to Nancy Dorian, because of a linguistic Social Darwinism which incorporates an ideology of contempt for languages without esteem, wealth, or power (1998:12). Haida, as a language, is resurfacing from a period in Canadian history when all languages except English and French were seen as contemptible. Even today, among some elders, Haida still remains a taboo language to speak as a result of assimilationist efforts that viewed English (in the case of the Haida) as superior and Haida as inferior.

Coupled with this ideology is an approach to teach less dominant or endangered languages in manner inconsistent with the students' world view. This approach gives preferentiality to "reference," that is words for things, to the point of fetishizing reference. One important danger of this approach is differences between languages are greatly diminished, and ultimately the only distinction is that words for the same thing are different. Endangered language lessons tend to focus only on nouns or adjectives, but do not allow or integrate the students' own world view or culture within the lessons in order to understand and effectively use the new words they are learning. All too often, certain aspects of the language's structure are privileged over the language's actual use. Kroskrity notes that in such a view, language is epiphenomenal, removed from the social structures and processes as well as cultural artifacts and activities produced by members; it thus merely reflects the "real" world. (2000:347)

The Haida language program must avoid such ideologies if the Haida language is to be revitalized within their communities. One key to this effort is to have esteem for the Haida language coupled within Haida identity. Dorian's observation concerning language and identity serves as a warning as she writes,

> The question of linkage between a language and the culture it's associated with becomes so delicate a matter that it's almost easier to insist on the importance of language to heritage and identity in settings where the ancestral language is entirely lost than in settings where it's retained by a relatively small number. (1998:21)

It is insightful as a warning, but it may also be taken as an exhortation or encouragement which the Haida community can embrace to foster their goal to achieve daily usage of the Haida language once again.

Appendix A
Excerpt of 1994 First Grade Class

001 D: okay, you got it all down↑

002 ":   as much as you can get↑

003 Casey: <u>not me</u>

004 H Sara: yep

005 D: and then I get somebody

006 ":   to come up

007 ":   and draw for me ((OK)

008 Casey: me {hand raised and waving}

009 Ann: I'll do *saablii* (bread)

010   ":   I'll do *saablii*   {hand raised and waving}

011   ":   I'll do *saablii*   {hand raised and waving}

012 Dawn: I'm *guud* (eagle) {hand raised and waving}

013 Hope: I'm *gyuu*. (ear)...<u>oo::hh::</u> {hand raised and waving}

014 Ann: *saablii*   {hand raised and waving}

015 D: why don't I start with *daaws* ↑ (cat)

016   ":   with Kate

017 Ka: {Horizontal Head Shake--HHS }

018 Jane: <u>Me</u>   {hand raised and waving}

019 D: no↑ {HHS looking at Kate}

020 Casey: I'll do it

021 D: okay, *daaws* (cat)

022 Jane: me {hand raised and waving}

023 D: *daaws* (cat) is↑ {points at the blackboard}

024 H Sara: cat

025 Jake: I'll do *xaa* (dog)

026 D: okay

027 Jake: I'll do *xaa* (dog)

```
028  D:            okay
029  H  Jason:     I'll do that house
030  D:            okay
031  Jane:         I'll do saablii (bread)
032  Frank:        I'll do house
033  Jane:         I'll do saablii (bread)
034  H Jason:      I'm doing house
035  Hope:         I'll do gyuu
036  Jake:         I'll do xaa (dog)
037  Students:     ((too much noise))
038  Jake:          xaa (dog)
039  H  Jason:     could I do ↑{hesitates}
040  Jake:         I'm doing xaa (dog)
041  Frank:        I am..
042  Jake:         I am..
043  SG4:          I am gyuu (ear)
044  Jane:         I am..
045  D:            oh.. good..
046  ":            what is it in English↑
047  Hope:         cat
048  H Sara:       ((cat))
049  D:            do you know how to spell cat?
050  Hope:         {nods affirmatively}
051  D:            okay, can you write cat up there↑
052  Jane:         I know [ how to spell cat
053  D:                   ]okay [ {to inquiring student}
054  H Jason:             ] Dora↑ (0.5) Dora↑ [
055       ":                                 ] [Dora, can I do the house↑
056       ":                                 ]{walking to instructor}
057  Jane:         can I do saablii ↑  (bread)
```

058	H Jason:	can [I do the house↑
059	":	]{standing beside blackboard gazing at the instructor}
060	D:	okay, uhmm {watching the board}
061	":	{glances twice at the boy}
062	Jane:	((can I do bread)) ↑
063	":	can I do *saablii* ↑(bread)
064	":	can I do *saablii* ↑
065	":	can I do *saablii*↑
066	":	can I do *saablii*↑
067	H Jason:	I get to do hou:se[
068	":	]{turns around to go back to his seat}
069	Jane:	can I do *saablii* ↑ (bread)
070	D:	okay, Katie will do *saablii*
071	Jane:	oo::hh::
072	SG4:	I'm *gyuu* (ear)
073	students:	((laughter))
074	D:	That's a good one
075	":	can you put↑
076	":	can you write↑
077	":	can you write up there↑ {pointing at the blackboard}
078	Jake:	*xaa*↑ (dog)
079	D:	yeah, in English
080	students:	((laughter)
081	H Sara:	dog
082	Jake:	I know that
083	SG4:	Looks like a ((den)) woman
084	D:	GOOD, that's a good job {to Katie}
085	Jane:	what ((unclear) Katie, put bread, bread
086	D:	okay okay Katie write it
087	":	right here {pointing to the board}

088 Jane: I know how to spell bread

089 H Charles: Don]

090 Jane: [no, not red,] put bread] on it

091 D: [B

092 H Charles:] Don [

093 D:] R [

094 H Charles:] Don

095 D: E

096 Jane: put bread on it

097 D: A [

098 Jane:] *saablii,* [((bread))

099 D:] D [

100 Jane:] *saablii* (bread)

101 H Charles: Don

102 H Don: What↑

103 Jane: bread

104 D: good good

105 Jane: Lorna, can I ((do/draw) the *na* (house)

106 D: okay {points to the board}

107 Jane: {goes to the board and draws a house}

108 H Sara: ((asks a question))

109 D: she is doing *na* (house) right now

110 ":   {looking at Jane and pointing at Jane/board}

111 H Jason: {Stands up}

112 H Sara: Jason's doing that

113 D: O::h I forgot Jason's supposed to do house

114 H Jason: {begins to walk up front but stops at a desk}

115 D: [Hey,

116 H Sara:] Jason

117 D: Jason can you draw me a *gyuu*↑ (ear) [

118 ":   ]{looks at Jason}

119 H Jason: {begins walking to the board}

120 D: then *gyuu,* for ear, can you do that↑ {stands erect}

121 H Sara: ((you got to spell house though)) {comment to Jane}

122   ":   {provides the letters} o....u....s....e

123 H Jason: {goes to the board and looks and finds chalk}

124   [yeah I'll draw *gyuu* (ear)

125   ]{standing at the board putting a finger in his ear}

126 D: That's a good ear {comments on Jason drawing}

127 ":   ((1.2)) that's a re::al good ear

Appendix B
Skidegate 1994 1st grade class

1	D:	we have done just to see if you remember
2	":	do you
3	?"	*saablii* (bread)
4	S1:	((yelping noise))
5	S2:	heh heh
6	D:	whose is this↑
7	S1:	oh
8	S2:	Andrew
9	?:	Andrew
10	S3:	Andrew
11	S4:	Hey Dora↑
12	S5:	that's my favorite
13	S6:	Sara
14	D:	Yes
15	S:	Over here
16	D:	Oh ((laughs))
17	S1:	I don't know
18	S2:	Derrick
19	?:	yours
20	S3:	yeah
21	S4:	Eric
22	D:	could I help you↑
23	S1:	okay we going to draw one two three four four eight pictures please
24	S2:	on a blank page
25	S3:	Eric and Lester
26	S4:	oh cool
27	D:	draw them on a page

125

28	":	OKAY what were going to do first
29	":	I want you to draw first is
30	":	*daaws* (cat)
31	S:	*daaws* (cat)
32	D:	yeah don't say it just draw it
33	S1:	just draw it
34	S2:	I know what it is cat
35	D:	yes draw your lines
36	":	*daaws* (cat)
37	S1:	Yes I'd like you to draw a *daaws* but don't tell anyone
38	S2:	*daaws* (cat)
39	S3:	I have one
40	S4:	I have one
41	S5:	I have one
42	S6:	it's not mine
43	D:	don't tell each other kay *daaws* (cat)
44	S1:	I have no *daaws* (cat)
45	S2:	I like *daaws* (cat) though
46	S3:	I have a *daaws* I have a *daaws* I have a *daaws* (cat)
47	S4:	I have a *daaws* (cat) at home
48	S5:	my brother has a *daaws* (cat)
49	S6:	I have a *daaws* (cat) at home
50	D:	oh gee is that right-write the Haida word down
51	S1:	I don't know what a *daaws*(cat) is
52	S2:	Oh I know what a *daaws* (cat) is
53	S3:	meow
54	D:	what else...what is this *xaa*↑ (dog)
55	S:	Yea
56	D:	draw a *xaa* (dog) and just leave it and write the Haida name down
57	":	I I'll put the answers up after draw a *xaa* (dog)

58	?"	don't tell her
59	D:	you told her
60	?:	its got four legs
61	D:	don't copy hers either
62	S1:	a horse
63	S2:	oh I know
64	S:	oh a dog
65	D:	remember nice *xaa* (dog) nice *xaa* make a *xaa* too
66	S:	I know what that is it's a *gyuu* (ear)
67	D:	uh huh
68	S:	horse
69	D:	don't tell each other
70	S1:	horse
71	S2:	horse
72	S3:	I didn't hear
73	D:	good very good I'll look at my paper
74	S1:	gee you're bad
75	S2:	gee you're bad
76	D:	draw a *guud guud* (eagle)
77	S:	*guud* (eagle)
78	D:	you've had that one *guud guud* (eagle)
79	S1:	actually
80	S2:	I really close
81	D: we have two clans we have raven & we have eagle guess which one this is
82	S1:	raven
83	S2:	eagle
84	S3:	eagle
85	D:	uh huh
86	S1:	eagle
87	S2:	raven

88	D:	uhhm put ears on it and a nose and tail and a four legs
89	S:	*guud* (eagle)
90	D:	draw your *guud guud* (eagle)
91	S:	I'm not sure which one to draw
92	D:	draw one for me
93	?:	the black board
94	D:	I'm just trying to make it plain
95	S:	I'm not a very good artist but I'll try
96	D:	ah there's the one you want
97	":	*saablii* (bread)
98	S:	ohh
99	D:	yeah
100	S1:	too easy
101	S2:	too too easy
102	D:	you remember what *saablii* (bread) is↑
103	S1:	it's too easy
104	S2:	bread
105	D:	well you know them all that's good
106	S:	not all of them not the *gyuu* (ear)
107	D:	try to make I'll do one that's maybe is not so easy for you
108	S1:	no no no no no no no
109	S2:	is not
110	S3:	is too
111	S4:	but I can't draw it
112	S5:	I know what it is but I can't draw it very well
113	D:	draw a *na* (house)
114	S:	I know what it is
115	D:	okay good draw a *na* (house) for me
116	S1:	I'm done
117	S3:	it's a house

118	D:	uh uh draw draw a *na* (house) for me
119	S1:	it's a house
120	S2:	it's a house
121	D:	then I am going to ask each one of you to come a draw for me
122	S1:	no way
123	S2:	yes way
124	S3:	could you pick me for *daaws*↑ (cat)
125	D:	okay
126	S1:	could you pick me ↑
127	S2:	can you pick me ↑
128	S3:	could you pick me for *xaa*↑ (dog)
129	S4:	*xaa* (dog)
130	S5:	I'm *xaa* (dog)
131	S4:	I'm *xaa* (dog)
132	S5:	okay I'm *saablii* (bread)
133	S6:	pick me for *saablii* (bread)
134	S7:	I'm *daaws* (cat)
135	D:	draw a *gyuu* remember what a *gyuu* (ear) is↑
136	S:	oh yeah ear
137	D:	body part
138	S1:	ohhhh
139	S2:	what is it↑
140	D:	body part
141	S1:	ear
142	S2:	ear
143	D:	body part
144	S1:	there's no body
145	S2:	I didn't draw arms...
146	S3:	ohh
147	D:	ohh draw what you think it is

148 S1: I know what it is
149 S2: a *gyuu* (ear)
150 D: I think a lot of you know what a *gyuu* (ear) is it's a body part
151 D: e a r
152 ((Expanded transcript in Appendix A for this section))
153 S1: look I'm using my bread for
154 S2: gab
155 D: e a r
156 S1: I got all of them right
157 S2: I got all of them right you copied me in the middle
158 D: e a r
159 D: who wants to draw *guud*↑ (eagle)
160 S1: *guud* (eagle)
161 S2: <u>me</u>
162 S3: <u>me me</u>
163 D: who didn't have a turn↑
164 S: Meka
165 D: Meka
166 S1: me
167 S2: that's a lot
168 D: *guud guud* what is a *guud* ↑ (eagle)
169 S: eagle
170 D: okay
171 S1: here I did one
172 S2: oooh oooh
173 S3: *xaa* (dog)
174 D: come over here
175 S: ah ah ah a;
176 D: yeah you could try
177 S1: look at mine I only did

178	S2:	yeah nice drawing
179	S3:	holy
180	D:	good eagle very good
181	S1:	cool
182	S2:	how did he know what to↑
183	D:	*guud*
184	S1:	eagle e-a-g-l-e
185	S2:	brother one two three
186	D:	put the Haida words on them okay please
187	S:	four five
188	D:	good good eagle
189	S1:	my house is
190	S2:	yeah
191	S3:	yeah
192	?:	Jason
193	S4:	I'm gonna color mine all in
194	D:	okay you could color them now
195	D:	very good
196	S1:	we get to color them in now
197	S2:	I'm gonna color my dog black
198	D:	okay
199	S1:	how about my ears↑
200	S2:	green
201	S3:	I'm...
202	S4:	black
203	S5:	I'm gonna color them green
204	D:	((laughs)) green ears ((laughs))
205	S1:	I'm trying to
206	S2:	excuse me I black
207	S3:	it looks like green

208	D:	nice eagle hey↑
209	S1:	draw the ear black
210	S2:	draw the ear purple
211	D:	draw the ear
212	S:	draw the ear black
213	D:	June would you like to do your own↑
214	S1:	remember last time↑
215	S2:	no
216	S3:	no no
217	D:	very good eagle
218	S1:	.owww...
219	S2:	eagle
220	S3:	Dora Dora,
221	D:	what are you looking for↑
222	S1:	Dora,
223	S2:	Dora, Dora,
224	S3:	no wait I'm a zombie
225	S4:	a yellow cat
226	S5:	yellow
227	S6:	a zombie with the things
228	S7:	Dan,
229	D:	good drawing
230	D:	Dan, Dan, Dan
231	S1:	Daryl's pencil
232	S2:	what↑
233	S3:	Daryl's pencil
234	D:	that's my pencil
235	S:	good...
236	D:	nice drawing
237	S1:	hhhh give it

238	S2:	ouch
239	S3:	Daryl took my pencil
240	S4:	all right
241	S5:	oh yeah
242	S6:	((unclear))
243	S7:	oh yeah
244	S8:	((unclear))
245	S9:	I'm gonna cut it in half
246	S10:	Oh oh Oh oh
247	S11:	ah ah ah ah
248	S12:	give me the pencil
249	S13:	go ahead
250	S14:	ear
251	S15:	here that's dog that's cat that's eagle that's...
252	S16:	give me the pencil
253	MT:	Jenny put the Haida names on it okay so next time you'll know
254	D:	oh nice
255	S:	I'm done
256	D:	hey Jason why you didn't wait↑ {looking at him}
257	":	put the Haida names on all your pictures {pointing to the papers}
258	S:	here's here's
259	D:	and then you'll know okay↑ okay
260	S:	now it's *xaa* (dog)
261	D:	Katie {looking at her craft}
262	":	wait wait you need something else there
263	S:	I know I got it in the
264	D:	it's too early yet two more minutes
265	S:	cause I'm just going to put it on the desk
266	D:	did you put the Haida names under them↑
267	S:	no

268	S:	chee awesome computer man
269	D:	Katie
270	MT:	did you put the Haida names under them↑
271	S1:	look they're up there okay
272	S2:	((laughter))
273	D:	Jessica
274	G:	yes
275	S:	ow
276	D:	good drawing good drawing how are you doing↑
277	S:1	good
278	S2:	back
279	S3:	I'm gonna kick you in the shins
280	S4:	I'm gonna kick you in the shins
281	S5:	((laughter))
282	D:	put your names on them okay↑ John
283	S1:	where's the pencil jar↑
284	S2:	aaaahh
285	S3:	where's the pencil jar↑
286	D:	put it on the board okay↑
287	S:	right there
288	D:	who needed help↑
289	S:	oh cool
290	D:	you need some help↑
291	S1:	can you help me↑
292	S2:	ear do you know what ear is↑
293	S3:	*gyuu* (ear)
294	MT:	where's the pencil he is talking about↑ and yours someone is going
295	":	to find on the floor somewhere you know what that means though↑
296	":	it means that okay it is yours it is yours and you are getting it back,
297	":	but the question is let's keep on our places if this fell on the floor

298	":	up there kay that's understandable then
299	S:	Hey
300	MT:	but let's not
301	S:	Hey
302	MT:	if it is yours
303	S:	Darin
304	MT:	if it was your pencil then uhhm Katie you did nothing wrong, so you
305	":	know so the pencil there if it was your pencil, you know you would
306	":	back too so it's only fair to give it back okay
307	S:	get it Darin Darin look
308	D:	what↑
309	S1:	three o'clock
310	S2:	I put all my stuff
311	MT:	all of you up there at the board can you get down↑
312	D:	yes you can
313	S:	there
314	D:	can you erase that↑
315	S:	oh no oh no
316	MT:	Willie and Joseph
317	S:	oh no no
318	D:	Jason
319	S1:	I'm not
320	S2:	Mr. Kaffey
321	D:	Jason
322	S:	I think you're okay
323	D:	Chris are you using this↑
324	S1:	Mr. Kaffey
325	S2:	don't erase it
326	S3:	yeah yeah
327	S4:	I'll tell you what I am

328	S5:	I'm *gyuu* (ear)
329	S6:	I'm a
330	S7:	ohh
331	S8:	uhhm
332	S9:	house
333	S10:	Don Don
334	D:	okay
335	S1:	Sharon
336	S2:	you dropped that on purpose
337	MT:	there's no time for board games there's no time for board games
338	":	because Haida finishes in about two minutes
339	D:	thank you
340	?:	are you finished↑
341	S1:	what↑
342	?:	are you finished↑
343	S2:	hold it hold it
344	MT:	put everything back
345		Lesson is over

Appendix C

1st grade crafts Skidegate 12/98

01	G:	go ahead you'll see it sitting in [
02	SHG1:	]which office↑
03	SG:	Ben
04	SHG2:	can I go with her↑
05	G:	pardon↑
06	SHG2:	I can help her↑
07	G:	sure
08	SHG1:	I know where they are
09	G:	you know what the pencil case looks like↑ you'll see them in our
10	":	mailboxes the teacher's mailboxes {girls leave the room}
11	G:	girls {leaving the room} in Pam's office
12	S1:	you know that uhmm↑
13	SHB:	what do I got to do↑
14	S1:	that Jesus
15	G:	{walking back in classroom} you gotta dance with me {dancing}
16	SHB:	no {horizontal head shake}
17	Ss:	{laughter}
18	SB:	yeah you got to dance with her if you gonna[
19	SG:	][no he didn't
20	SB:	]be right ((Steph)) said
21	S1:	give Alward
22	S2:	except me
24	S3:	except create ((except for me))
25	S4:	yeah
26	G:	what's that↑
27	S:	{repeats but unclear}
28	G:	then its right here hey↑

29 S: {nods her head}

30 G: stop right here did you do one of these↑ {going through paper on desk}

31 S: yes

32 G: {reading names on papers}Emmy Tylor that has no name Kamila and then

33 ": there's this one that has no name Raven Kamila did you do a swallow↑

34 K: yeah

35 G: then it's right here hey {holding it up in the air}

36 ":   can you do a wheel↑

37 S: where's my what↑

38 G: I think I gave it away Emily that has two more and there's this one

39 ":   with two more

40 S: I did one I did mine

41 Ss: {girls return from the office with the pencils}

42 G: good gee you girls are smart ((2.0)) {taking the pencils from girls}

43 ":   kay Donald here they are ((shaking the colored pencils))

44 S: Megan

45 T: or anybody else who needs these and this is for you{gives pencil to student}

46 S: no

47 G: I just need to wait for Mrs. Forsay to come back so I can run to the laminator

48 S: she is back

49 G: Pardon↑

50 S1:   she is back

51 S2:   we can take care of ourselves

52 SG: I am going to erase this head ((erases the chalk board))

53 TA: leave the sign

54 SG: this hand is too much work

55 G: you guys have a very good teacher

56 ":   what should I put on your guys' tree↑

57 S1:   a stocking

58 SGH: a snowman

59	G:	<u>oh </u>I already did a snowman something <u>different</u>
60	S1:	I know
61	SHB:	a Santa Claus
62	G:	okay a Santa Claus and a what↑
63	S1:	and reindeer
64	S2:	yeah
65	SBH:	yeah
66	G:	no a tiny reindeer
67	S1:	I'm Santa he's a reindeer
68	S2:	he's big
69	G:	I love these ((1.0)) I missed Alexis
70	SBH:	I'll tell you what <u>I am</u> I'm a toy soldier
71	G:	yeah you should put a toy soldier on it
72	S1:	yeah
73	S2:	no
74	S3:	yeah
75	G:	put a small soldier
76	S:	no
77	G:	on one and on the other
78	S:	I just did an elephant
79	G:	Jane you need to turn around and do your work
80	Ja:	{turns around}
81	S:	can we do a soldier↑
82	G:	because these need to be done before next week {waving at Katie}
83	":	<u>HI</u> Katie you want to see the kids↑ come on come and see all the kids
84	K:	{comes in with her aid}
85	G:	at a girl boy she's good {to the aid} you looked bored
86	K:	{walking towards a desk}
87	G:	say hi to all the kids
88	TA2:	say hi can you say hi↑

89	K:	{stopping at Ronald's desk}
90	G:	that's my boy Ronald he's my baby
91	S:	yeah
92	G:	this is the grade one class oh you want to come sit down↑
93	K:	yeah
94	U:	{Genie and TA together} yeah
95	TA2:	{laughs} you want to be joined right in here
96	G:	oh oh , should I get you a chair↑ {goes to back of the room for a chair}
97	TA2:	she's getting kind a big for those desks
98	K:	{squirming into a desk}
99	G:	yeah I don't think you can fit in them
100	TA2:	she says I'm gonna try
101	K:	{sits in the desk}
102	G:	oh she is going to oh gee you're tricky
103	U:	{laughter}
104	G:	is that your desk↑
105	S:	that's Kam's
106	U:	{laughter}
107	G:	are you uncomfortable in there↑
108	K:	{Horizontal HEAD SHAKE}
109	TA2:	are you in grade one↑
110	U:	{laugher}
111	G:	she wants to relax hey↑
112	S:	ha ha Kamila
113	TA2:	she is not you want to relax hey↑
114	G:	you want to color a snowman↑ huh↑
115	K:	((horizontal head shake))
116	G:	you just want to sit there↑
117	K:	{nods her head horizontal head shake}
118	TA2:	she just joined in {laughter}

119 MT: oh well

120 TA2:   picked out a desk and plopped down {laughter}

121 G: kind of nice here hey↑ this is Sandra {pointing to girl beside her}

122 K: ((ooooh))

123 G: say hi to Sandra

124 TA2:   say hi

125 TA: just pieces of this box and stick it to that

126 G: I'm going to run these through the laminator real quick I'll be right back

127 :"   you guy find some ((unclear)) board {leaves the class}

128 MT: no ((unclear)) together

129 G: oh okay

130 T: Kamila

131 TA2:   she is sitting here are you ready to go↑

132 MT: oh there you go

133 TA2:   a rug rat Rusty the rugrat

134 TA: well you can't stay in grade one when you're in high school

135 S: the guy with a little planet on his shirt

136 TA: got to finish the attendance

137 MT: on the next week

138 TA: yep

139 U: {laughter}

140 D: oh Denver

141 TA2:   what's your name↑

142 SB: Brandon

143 TA2:   I know you're Brandon

144 SB: Brandon

145 TA2:   Brendon

146 SB: Brandon

147 TA2:   oh you're Brandon too okay

148 G: {walking back into the class} okay friends let's go

149 S: ((what's that)) ↑

150 G: it's magic it does what I tell it to do

151 S: ((unclear response))

152 G: I won't do it then look what Andra brought

153 TA2: we'll take it with us and then you can bring it back come on {to Katie}

154 G: once you get these cut out your circles again and make sure they are all

155 ":facing upright {stops} Valerie and fold them in half and staple them together

156 S: Lisa↑

157 G: you need help↑ were you back here↑ oh my they're so cute

158 MT: {chuckle} these are cute

159 G: yeah

160 TA2: come on

161 G: she's enjoying us

162 G: Ashely

163 S: no way

164 G: David

165 D: when you cut that out I'll help you make it

166 S: apple

167 D: what

168 G: boy you barely made it

169 ":   *howaa* (thank you)

170 TA2: good girl

171 S: ohh

172 G: so you better get busy

173 ":   *howaa* (thank you) for dropping in

174 Ss: {laughter}

175 D: gee that's warm

176 S: {asking a question about a paper}

177 G: okay that's for Andra {looking for Andra} hey Paul there wasn't

178 ":   one here for you

179	S:	I never remember him
180	G:	you want to look in that pile[
181	S:	][remember that ((unclear))
182	G:	]because there are a couple with no names
183	":	{pointing up front} right there
184	S:	{starts walking to the pile}
185	TA:	oh oh oh
186	G:	if not grab another one of these {pointing to a stack on the pile}
187	S:	{from the back of the class} everybody look
188	T:	Reagan
189	G:	((gasp)) pretty you did a beautiful job {walking to back of class}
190	G:	way to go good going Ashley((3.5))okay you all need to go to your seats
191	Ss:	{three students walk back to their seats}
192	S1:	book
193	S2:	((3.0)) chair
194	G:	oh okay
195	E:	{shuffling and talking to much noise to hear clearly}
196	D:	Ellen oh
197	Do:	mommy I'm done
198	S1:	what the↑
199	S2:	where did you come from↑
200	G:	ok you need to color the holly then color the other stuff
201	D:	{goes back to his seat}
202	Ss:	{getting very loud}
203	G:	oh oh oh we're getting too loud {walks to back of the class} ((3.0))
204	S:	Donald you're not ((done))
205	Ss:	{too loud again}
206	G:	here's the scissors
207	S1:	I know
208	S2:	whose is that that gold guy↑

209	G:	that's Linus'
210	S:	DALLAS
211	Ss:	{too loud to hear clearly} ((25.0))
212	D:	now you need to fold it in half
213	S:	yeah
214	G:	that's too high hey ((3.6)) that's too high
215	Ss:	{all have stopped working on the Christmas stuff}
216	G:	okay friends {walking to front with the newly laminated papers}
217	Ss:	{two girls follow her to the front}
218	MT	clean up
219	SH:	{runs to his desk}
220	MT:	clean up
221	G:	Where are the↑
222	S1:	Teacher
223	S2:	Mrs. Foresay↑
224	MT:	you guys go and sit down and do your Haida stuff
225	D:	Dallas Dallas {walking towards Dallas}
226	G:	cut these out and I make a ball for you
227	D:	fold it in half
228	":	Yes yes Brendon
229	MT:	When you finish your Haida ornaments here's a Christmas coloring
230	":	contest but you have to finish your Haida ornaments first
231	D:	Dallas Dallas Dallas Dallas I asked you to ((unclear))
232	":	{focuses on the craft for a minute}
233	Ss:	{loud and boisterous} ((15.0))
234	G:	Ronald don't play with that you might wreck it okay↑
235	Do:	okay mom it won't fall off
236	Ss:	{louder and restless}
237	G:	okay now who's the fourth soldier↑
238	SBs:	{two boys with a red garland put it around the Christmas tree}

239 Ss: {continue loud and boisterous}

240 G: uhmm Ronald and Kyle you need to finish your work Ronald you

241 ":   need to finish yours

242 K: {walks up to Janey}

243 G: kay quick

244 K: I'm putting it in[

245 G:]no go finish your thing because we don't have much time left

246 S: {from the back of the room} what are these↑

247 MT: {from the back of the room} what ever it is it's too big for you

248 Ss: {laughter and loudness playing with sticks}

249 D: Dallas and Kamila sit down and color put those away

250 D&K: {both sit down}

251 K: I need help

252 D: {sits down beside her and starts coloring} I'll help you

253 S: sh::   sh {someone tries to quiet the students}

254 SBs: {pretending to fight with swords}

255 D: Dallas and Donald sit down and color put those away HEY

256 G: Donald did you finish yet↑

257 D: DALLAS AND DONALD Dallas that's the fourth Dallas time I'm

258 ":   talking to you

259 Do: and me

260 D: and you

261 G: {walks towards them from the back of class} yeah and get me mad real

262 ":   soon

263 D: color nice pictures we want to laminate them so you take them home

264 SB: like this↑

265 G: {goes back to talk to Mainstream teacher then both walk up to the

266 ":   students}

267 MT: Angie can I have a talk over here↑

268 Ss: {turn around and are quiet} ((2.5))

269 A: {gets out of her seat and walks to the back of the room}

270 SB: {screams}

271 MT: shh Brian who's the other one↑

272 AH: Reagan

273 S: Reagan

274 MT: Reagan too {walking to the back}

275 SB: {running to the back} I'm a ((unclear)) I'm a ((unclear)) I'm a

276 MT: There is green yellow red and blue

277 S1:   I want blue

278 S2:   blue

279 D: boy that's nice

280 MT: want color ((unclear))↑ want red green or yellow↑

281 S: green

282 MT: Reagan what color do you want↑

283 R: red

284 MT: okay

285 ?:   {from off camera} go sit down

286 D: make sure your name's on it

287 S1:   Stacey's here

288 S2:   Stacey your late I was late too

289 St: I know

290 S3:   you missed you missed Haida

291 MT: {from the corner } would you like to help with that please↑

292 S: I'm an ice-cream maker

293 G: who was red↑

294 S1:   red was Reagan

295 S2:   in Kindergarten ((unclear))

296 G: {walking to the front} you got a pony tail in your hair

297 D: are you finished↑ it's almost recess

298 Ss: {getting more and more restless as recess gets closer}

299 G: Dallas to your desk

300 S: ((unclear))

301 G: Dallas in your desk and don't even move from there again put your

302 ": name on that and put it in my folder {walking to the back with a chair}

303 Do: mommy

304 G: make sure you clean up your mess Donald before you go out

305 Ss: ((loud and unclear))

306 G: Friends we need to start cleaning up

307 . . . . Lesson is over

Appendix D
1st grade crafts #2 Skidegate 12/98

1		Class is already started
2	D&G:	{handing out posters}
3	G:	oh Adriela's here {walking over and giving her a poster}
4	S:	{to another classmate} yeah it has your name on it
5	G:	Anita's here {gives her a poster}
6	S:	what color are you going to do the background↑
7	G:	here after you finish doing this you can do this {showing more crafts}
8	?:	{knocking at the door}
9	G:	{looking at the door} one moment I'm still doing it
10	S:	where did Kelsey's go↑ where did Kelsey's go↑
11	G:	just put your name right here {pointing on the paper}
12	D:	I'll go put the laminator on hey Genie↑ {leaving the class}
13	G:	I turned it on already
14	D:	oh did you↑ {walking back in to the class and around to the students}
15	":	holy that's nice coloring {pointing to the poster}
16	S1:	yeah
17	S2:	this one stinks
18	S3:	no
19	S4:	you forgot
20	S5:	go look for dolphin
21	D:	yes you can
22	G:	Are you finished↑ we're going to cut them out and put them on paper
23	D:	holy you're rich what is that↑ is that an eraser↑
24	S:	right here
25	G:	Brandon here's the wool
26	S1:	give it
27	S2:	give it to me

28 G: Val you want to grab her wool↑{looking at her}oh and you're here too

29 S1:　　　Bobby↑

30 S2:　　　scissors

31 G: sorry {to person off camera waiting for attendance slip}I'm a little

32 ":bit slow today ((2.5)) I need something for oh here comes Karol and Luke

33 D:　　　I'll be right back I need to[

34 S:　　　　　　　　　　　　　][I need a pencil

35 D:　　　　　　　　　　　　　] to phone

36 G:　　　after you step out I need to get some work done

37 D:　　　oh that's okay Kari is there

38 G:　　　{leaves the classroom}

39 D:　　　holy what nice runners you have they're nice

40 S1:　　is this red↑

41 ?:　　　okay I'll show you

42 S2:　　I remember

43 S3:　　Bobby's here too

44 D:　　　I'll let Sonny know you're here

45 G:　　　okay boys I want you to stay in your desks

46 S:　　　well you're showing everyone

47 G:　　　stay in your desks

48 SB:　　shiver me timbers

49 D:　　　boy I'm hungry today

50 G: does anybody have a pair of scissors↑ Jake can I borrow some scissors↑

51 J:　　　{gives her the scissors}

52 G:　　　okay there you go Tyson {gives the scissors to Tyson}

53 SB:　　I have to go up to the office

54 S1:　　oh me too

55 S2:　　me three

56 G:　　　why↑

57 S:　　　it's a good hard knot

58	SB:	to give pennies
59	G:	anybody also got any pennies↑
60	Ss:	<u>me me</u>
61	G:	would it be all right if he takes your pennies down↑
62	SB:	nobody's taking these down
63	G:	Okay you can take em by yourself then
64	S:	it's a hard knot
65	G:	okay boys walk down to the office quietly
66	SBs:	{start walking out of the class}
67	G:	walk down to the office quietly and give your pennies
68	SB:	I did it I did it the way you said I should do it
69	G:	good now put it over here and grab some wool
70	SB:	the way you said I should do it
71	D:	oh don't even have to {to Genie}
72	G:	I'm making poinsettias for my door
73	S1:	it's a cat
74	S2:	{gags} I hate ((unclear))
75	G:	I want it to look beautiful
76	S1:	beautiful
77	S2:	could I see the blue one↑
78	Ss:	{getting too loud to hear clearly}
79	G:	you have to be quiet because Ms. Doffy is really out in the hallway
80	S1:	don't try for Laura Ms. Laura
81	S2:	on my
82	S3:	I'm writing second
83	S4:	I'm writing last
84	S5:	this
85	G:	okay you can grab wool
86	D:	okay Karol keep coloring
87	G:	okay who has the pair of scissors I can use↑

88	S:	I do
89	G:	*howaa* (thank you) Bobby
90	S1:	uh oh
91	S2:	<u>look it's raining</u>
92	S3:	oops
93	S4;	all one↑
94	G:	Asia you need to put that pack down there
95	Ss:	{too loud and confused to hear clearly} ((6.8))
96	D:	you got this↑ Bobby↑ Bobby↑
97	G:	Daria here's yours
98	S1:	do you have skinny purple↑ skinny purple↑ skinny purple↑
99	S2:	I have skinny purple
100	S3:	I needed a red
101	S4:	did you see the time when my things hopped over like this↑
102	S5:	{shakes his head}
103	S6:	it shot out
104	S7:	you can use fat too
105	D:	oh really nice
106	S1:	{groaning}
107	S2:	yellow and black yellow and black
108	D:	you can color any color you want
109	S1:	yeah↑
110	Ss:	{too loud to hear clearly}
111	G:	ooh I like this one
112	S:	bathroom
113	D:	yeah ((2.1)) gee that's pretty hey Genie↑ {comments on poster}
114	G:	take those down and put it a blue back on it
115	D:	((unclear)) for all of us Genie {laughs}
116	Ss:	{laugh as well}
117	G:	one of the teachers told me to save them for January

118	D:	oh that's good
119	G:	remember when we used to make↑
120	D:	that's pretty Genie {about a Christmas ornament then walks over to a
121	":	student} you got a bloody mouth↑ {looking in the girl's mouth}
122	Sg:	{girl nod's her head and opens her mouth for the instructor to see}
123	D:	{says something to the girl too low to hear}
124	Sg:	{girl gets up holding her mouth and leaves the class}
125	D:	{walks over and talks quietly to Genie}
126	G:	{walks to middle of classroom} mmm it smells like grapes in here
127	S1:	right here
128	S2:	oh I have the red ones
129	D:	{laughing}
130	G:	ohh that's why {looking the scented markers}
131	S1:	I got ((unclear flavor)) at home
132	S2:	I do too
133	S1:	I got the yellow one
134	S2:	no
135	S3:	any of them smell like ((unclear))
136	Ss:	no no
137	G:	kay we got to put these together next Thursday because next
138	":	Tuesday I'll be gone
139	S:	why↑
140	G:	I'll be fixing some hats for the Christmas concert
141	S1:	okay
142	S2:	scissors
143	G:	boy you're a smart cutter
144	G:	wow who taught you that↑ he he did his name in hand writing
145	D:	{looking at his poster}
146	S1:	sure
147	S2:	hey cool

148	S3:	look what's under it look what's under it
149	S4:	piece of paper
150	S5:	do you any fish↑
151	G:	do I have any fish↑
152	S:	yeah
153	G:	you mean at home↑
154	S:	no fish you eat
155	G:	why would you like one with salmon↑
156	S:	yeah
157	G:	I could make one specially for you
158	S:	okay I'll help
159	S:	I'll make one tomorrow
160	Ss:	we want one too
161	G:	I'll make it tonight and give it to you tomorrow
162	S1:	I want some salmon too
163	S2:	I do too
164	D:	are you lazy today↑
165	SB:	knock knock
166	S1:	who's there↑
167	SB:	elephant
168	S2:	elephant who
169	S3:	I've got a cold up my trunk
170	G:	{laughs}
171	?:	oh ((unclear))
172	G:	oh hi Kelsey did you just get here↑
173	K:	{shakes her head}no Ms. MaGouhgy
174	G:	oh Ms. Gouphy
175	S1:	MAGOUPHY
176	S2:	that's what ((you)) call her
177	S3:	oh yeah ((laughter))

153

178	D:	he came home at uhh he's home at 8:30
179	S1:	no you have black
180	S2:	no oh yeah I do
181	D:	oh cute
182	G:	yes
183	?:	but we have you know we have kids playing just quickly jump
184	G:	okay friends you have to put away the colors
185	S1:	I'll make
186	S2:	Luke Ania
187	G:	do you have a bleeding mouth↑
188	S:	yes
189	G:	did you lose a tooth↑
190	S:	no
191	G:	just wants to bleed huh↑
192	S:	pick up
193	D:	finished↑ my way here
194	G:	OKAY friends
195	S1:	we're not your friends
196	S2:	she's my friend
197	S3:	she's my friend
198	G:	someone here doesn't want to be my friend↑
199	S:	{student smiles}
200	Ss:	I do I do
201	SBs:	I don't I don't
202	G:	okay I'll see you all next Thursday
203	D:	thank you Kris
204	K:	that's okay
205	S1:	see you later alligator
206	S2:	in a while crocodile

Lesson is over

Appendix E
Skidegate 1st grade language and crafts mix

1	U:	*sgwaansing* (one) *sding* (two) *hlguunuhl* (three) *sdansing* (four)
2	":	*tlayhl* (five) *tlguunuhl* (six) *jiiguugaa* (seven) *sdangsingxaa* (eight)
3	":	*tlaahl gwii sgwaansing gaw* (nine) *tlaahl* (ten)
4	G:	good is Natalia having problems↑
5	S:	yeah
6	G:	in the foot area↑here{grabbing student's hair)Genie will help you I see
7	":	((1.0)) what you're trying to do ((4.0))
8	S1:	Peter where's Hasia↑ Hasia isn't here
9	S2:	yeah
10	G:	I was just wondering where she was
11	G:	hello
12	G:	you need to put the lego away
13	S:	Hasia's out there {pointing to the hallway}
14	G:	put put the lego away
15	S:	you got a big [
16	G:	][are we ready↑
17	SB:	] you got big stuff like that↑
18	S:	look it look it
19	SB:	castle
20	G:	can we all *gaaxaa hlaa* (stand) besides our seats please↑
21	S:	I got a castle
22	?:	yeah
23	G:	*gaaxaa hlaa* (stand) besides our seats please oh yeah good <u>boy</u> we listen well
24	Sg:	Aleks doesn't sit over here he sits there
25	G:	That's OK he's close enough are we ready↑
26	U:	yeah
27	U:	*kaajii xil 7ud* (touching their head and neck)
28	":	*kun 7ud xyaay* (chest and arms)

29	":	*kun 7ud xyaay*
30	":	*kun 7ud xyaay*
31	":	*kaajii xil 7ud kun 7ud xyaay*
32	":	*skwaay kwaay 7ud st'aay 7ud stl'aay* (touching back, feet hips & hands)
33	":	*sk'yaa'jii til 7ud skul 7ud kyaal* (Touching their eyebrows thighs)
34	":	*skul 7ud kyaal* (shoulders and legs)
35	":	*skul 7ud kyaal*
36	":	*sk'yaa'jii til 7ud skul 7ud kyaal*
37	":	*kul kun 7ud gyuu 7ud dul* (touching forehead, nose ear and stomach)
38	":	*xangii kuugaa* (touching their eyes and heart)
39	":	*tsing 7ud hlk'aay* (touching their teeth and chin)
40	":	*tsing 7ud hlk'aay*
41	":	*xangii kuugaa tsing 7ud hlk'aay*
42	":	*kuuluu skil 7ud* (touching their knees and bellybutton)
43	":	*xiihlii 7ud tlaats* (touching their mouth and top of the head)
44	":	*xaanga hlt'aa xuujii dogwul guudaa* (touching eyelashes and side)
45	":	*dogwul guudaa*
46	":	*dogwul guudaa*
47	":	*xaanga hlt'aa xuujii dogwul guudaa*
48	":	*kun kuntsii xul xiljii 7ud hluu* (touching front of body, lips, nostril & neck)
49	G:	*gaaw uu hlaa gaaw uu hlaa* (sit) sit down take your seats Aleks let's
50	":	swing back to this side because it is a little crowded on that on that end
51	AH:	I sat here already
52	MT:	no your seat is right there
53	AH:	my teacher wants me to sit here
54	G:	no I want you to swing back this way
55	AH:	yeah teacher said
56	SG:	{picking up and placing a chair near her} he sits over here
57	AH:	no teacher wants me here {pointing at his spot}
58	MT:	no this is your spot right here {coming pointing to place}

59	Sg:	and she sits here
60	MT:	Aleks
61	TA:	no
62	S:	Aleks yeah your spot is here
63	TA:	thank you
64	G:	great now let's do *dup'juu 7ul'juu* all together again okay
65	U:	*dup'juu 7ul'juu yang a jing* (tiny little spider)
66	":	{making hand motions for a spider}
67	":	went up the *gondl* (water) spout
68	":	{making crawling hand motions up in the air}
69	":	down came the *daala* (rain)
70	":	{making rain falling motions with their hands and fingers}
71	":	and washed the *yang a jing* (spider)
72	":	{making washing motions with their hands}
73	":	out came the *xaaya* (bubbles)
74	":	{making motions for bubbles with their hands to the sky}
75	":	and *gaagaa* (dried) all the *daala* (rain)
76	":	{making hand motions drying}
77	":	the *dup'juu 7ul'juu yang a jing* (little spider) went up the spout again
78	":	{making motions with their hands to indicate a spider climbing the spout}
79	G:	good who remembers how to say dog in Haida↑
80	S:	*xaa* (dog)
81	G:	*xaa* good what about cat↑
82	S:	*daaws* (cat)
83	G:	*dows* what about cow↑
84	S:	*moosmoos* (cow)
85	G:	what about horse↑
86	S:	*gyuudan* (horse)
87	G:	what about crab↑
88	S:	*k'uustan* (crab)

89	G:	what about frog↑
90	S:	*sgaaniinaa* (frog)
91	MT:	OK yeah
92	G:	what about butterfly↑
93	SBH:	*kulgaayuugwang* (butterfly)

94   G: good *kulgaayuugwang* <u>boy</u> that's a tough one to remember what about shrimp↑

95	SBH:	*guudgaagiigaayd* (shrimp)
96	G:	good what about pig↑
97	S:	*kobra* (pig)
98	G:	what about eagle↑
99	S:	*xuuya* (raven)
100	G:	what about eagle↑
101	S1:	*xuuya* (raven)
102	S2:	what about↑
103	G:	what is eagle↑
104	S:	*guud* (eagle)
105	G:	what is raven↑
106	SGH:	*xuuya* (raven)
107	S:	snake
108	G:	what about ↑ ((1.2)) I forgot one bear
109	S:	*taan* (bear)
110	G:	what about
111	S:	deer↑
112	G:	deer↑
113	S:	*gaat* (deer)
114	G:	rat↑
115	S1:	*kugan* (rat)
116	S2:	what was it↑
117	G:	*kugan kugan* a rat I didn't teach the afternoon kids those didn't I↑

118	S:	yeah

118 S: yeah
119 G: okay well we're going to continue on with our decorations so we can get
120 ": em done because I probably won't see you all next week you'll all be so busy
121 Ss: hhhh {gasping sounds}
122 S1: okay
123 S2: I love working
124 S3: yeah we're busy
125 S4: oh man
126 G   oh no {looking through her papers}
127 MT: you know what we are going to do↑
128 S: I like to make
129 G: oh yeah I have em I have em
130 TA: okay construction paper
131 MT: alright
132 S: okay
133 MT: Vonnie
134 S: hold on
135 MT: and they put the sticky things on there today
136 G: Tayler now you do the ((unclear)) okay
137 ":   Lila will you get Jenny all colors for the table please↑
138 D: yeah
139 G: *howaa* (thank you)
140 D: colors
141 G: there you go dear
142 TA: so I need em
143 S: he::y
144 G: shhhhh
145 MT: put it back on these
146 S: look
147 G: oh let's not put our shoes on the table

148	MT:	and if not if there's ((unclear))
149	G:	remember we need to stay in our own spot in our space
150	TA:	they due today ↑
151	MT:	yes
152	TA:	okay so what could I do here and then just keep that one in my box
153	G:	Pam did you start already↑
154	P:	what↑
155	TA:	just put it in your box
156	G:	oh no Pam Asia
157	TA:	OK
158	MT:	see you later
159	TA:	okay
160	G:	there you go ((Sterito))
161	S:	((fita))
162	G:	gee I miss Jace I haven't seen Jace for a while
163	S:	((rest))
164	G:	I have one here with no name on it I bet that belongs to
165	S:	you
166	G:	Natalia↑
167	TA:	no hers is cut out
168	G:	Mohammed it's not Kevin's Kevin's was
169	TA:	cut out that's uhmm
170	G:	Breeann's
171	TA:	or Pam
172	P:	no
173	G:	Is this yours Breeanne↑ here you go no name Asia's
174	S:	Passion's
175	TA:	is cut out if you don't is this whole things Raven's↑
176	G:	yeah
177	TA:	that's Harmonia's that's Harmonia's

178	G:	cause we need to glue these on the paper OK ((.07)) I'll get some paper
179	D:	where's your crayons Karol↑
180	S:	I'm going to get them
181	D:	okay go ahead
182	G:	Jason
183	SG:	I need to go pee
184	D:	Asia you need crayons↑
185	SG:	I need to go pee
186	G:	go then
187	D:	what are you looking for↑
188	TA:	I'll ((unclear))
189	G:	Krystyna you want crayons↑
190	K:	{nods her head}
191	G:	right beside you
192	TA:	Oh thank you Breeann
193	S:	Hey
194	TA:	where's your shoes↑
195	S:	my house
196	TA:	well when you get back put them on please
197	S:	Jenny
198	G:	yeah
199	S:	I think that I'm all finished
200	TA:	what you looking for↑
201	S:	whoa
202	SBH:	whoa {commenting on his stack of markers} look how many I have
203	TA:	finished↑
204	SB:	I have my own scissors you know ↑
205	G:	do you where'd you get em from↑
206	Sg:	ahh you
207	TA:	come on lets' color {dismantling the tower of markers}

208	SBH:	I used permanent ((markers)) for that
209	TA:	no you started with crayons Genie wants you to finish with crayons
210		OK↑
211	SBH:	look
212	TA:	all these color then we cut them out and finish them then we can start
213	":	another one OK↑
214	S1:	over here
215	S2:	yeah
216	TA:	OK you use these ones OK↑
217	S:	you have to cut them out
218	TA:	there you go
219	S:	permanent {speaking about markers}
220	G:	oh is that one permanent↑
221	S:	yeah
222	TA:	Krystyna where's your socks and shoes↑ {hands on mouth}
223	K:	{standing in silence}
224	TA:	hmmm↑ {bending over}
225	S1:	((giggle))
226	S2:	Raquel
227	TA:	pardon↑ where's your socks and shoes↑ in your bags↑
228	K:	{nods her head }
229	S:	hey
230	TA:	well how about we put them on please↑
231	SB:	guess what crayon↑
232	S:	Miss Genie I can't tell if this is crayon
233	TA:	that one's crayon these are all crayon Aleks
234	S:	this one I can't feel if its {playing with a crayon}
235	G:	OH Moses you didn't get one↑
236	S1:	I need a glue
237	S2:	teacher

238	G:	you want glue↑
239	S:	I have to cut them out
240	TA:	pardon↑
241	S:	you cut these out
242	TA:	you finish using the crayons here OK
243	G:	you want to do another one↑ OK go ahead if you wanna
244	TA:	((OK)) thank you
245	G:	I think aunty ran out
246	S:	why you run out↑
247	G:	uhhm somebody started a pink one
248	TA:	did Jenny say you could cut it out↑
249	S:	ahh
250	G:	Oh this is Mrs.Jordan's
251	TA:	pardon↑
252	S1:	I'm done
253	S2:	oh I can't find anything
254	G:	oh there's lots of colors {looking through a pile of papers}
255	S:	oh I wanted ((unclear))
256	G:	I think Kendall is more than happy to share
257	S:	and he gave me some ((Dome Kapers)) because he is my best friend
258	G:	you got (Kapers)↑
259	S:	he gave them to me
260	TA:	here let's move these over there to the trash can
261	G:	WOW
262	TA:	are you laminating these Genie↑
263	G:	yeah
264	TA:	let's move them over there
265	G:	Natalia you can finish Mrs. Jordan's
266	S:	HEY LOOK
267	G:	no↑ because auntie doesn't have more my dear {grabbing paper}

268 ": you got to be careful with the scissors you don't want to cut these right

269 S1: oh no

270 S2: no cause I ((got one))

271 G: because auntie doesn't have more ((2.0)) ahh my dear my dear my

272 ": dear {grabbing paper from student}you got to be careful with the

273 ": scissors you {sitting on her desk} don't want to cut these right

274 S: oh no

275 G: you want to keep in the circle {cutting the paper} look like this

276 TA: put them on the back of that one ((4.0))

277 S: mine where's mine↑

278 G: okay {cutting out the paper for the student} cause we want that circle

279 ": you fold along the black line okay↑ that's all we'll just make new

280 ": circles around this one {pointing at the paper}

281 AH: I did all ((this)) {holding his paper up to the instructor}

282 G: {looks at the paper and then back at the girl she was helping}

283 AH: now can I cut it out↑

284 G: {looking at the boy on her left}

285 AH: now can I cut it out↑

286 G: yes you may {starts to give him the scissors}

287 TA: there you go put some right here for me

288 AH: NO I have my own {starts cutting the paper and then sits down}

289 G: oh okay I have those back then {takes scissors stands to leave but

290 ": notices boy having problems} no no no no don't keep cutting right there

291 AH: what do I do↑

292 G: we want to cut the circles ((0.4)){grabs paper and cuts it for student}

293 TA: since Genie is going to take them to the laminator ((4.5))

294 G: yeah ((4.0))

295 TA: ((there some with on))

296 Sg: there is this good↑ {showing the craft to the instructor}

297 G:good girl{looking at craft}keep them in one place so you don't lose them

298	AH:	I'm keeping this in the lines
299	S:	((unclear calling to another student))
300	AH:	I'm keeping it right now
301	S:	I know that ((2.5)) I heard
302	TA:	are you finished coloring {taking away the crayons}
303	S:	yes another ((unclear)) ((3.0))
304	TA:	geez how many days til dad gets home↑ {to a student}
305	G:	it's this Friday
306	TA:	are you counting the days til dad gets home↑
307	Sg:	yeah
308	TA:	yeah ((3.5))
309	Ss:	((to noisy to hear))
310	TA:	okay ((2.8))
311	Sg:	guess what
312	G:	what↑
313	Sg:	I have my own diary
314	G:	you have your own diary↑
315	Sg:	I have a my uh uh my gallery
316	G:	you have a gallery↑
317	Sg:	yes
318	G:	oh my goodness
319	SB:	I've had for a long time
320	Ss:	((too hard to hear clearly)) ((43.0))
321	TA:	and then we are going to cover them with plastic (talking about
322	":	laminating the crafts}
323	G:	yeah we put plastic over them so they last ((2.0)) then you get to uhm
324	":	when you an adult ((you can say)) Oh I remember when I did this with
325	":	Ms. Genie in Kindergarten
326	Ss:	{looking at Genie} ((3.5))
327	G:	perfect

328	S:	what↑
329	G:	((2.3)) no I'm just looking for a circle {walking around the kind}
330	TA:	{grabbing the paper} careful see look Aleks cut on the black line
331	AH:	{watching her cut}
332	G:	whoops {laughs}
333	TA:	oh what happened↑ {walking over to the instructor}
334	G:	she was cutting the shape of the stars instead of the circles {fixing cut}
335	TA:	ohh ((6.3)){to Olek as he is cutting the paper} there you go ((4.4))
336	Sg:	what's this↑ ((8.0))
337	TA:	this whose is this one↑ {asking Aleks about a craft} okay
338	":	Aleks you want to cut this out↑
339	AH:	yeah
340	TA:	okay you need to cut on the black line not in it on the circle
341	S:	HEY COME BACK HERE ((too much noise to hear clearly)) ((9.4))
342	G:	I'm going to borrow can I borrow this ((1.2)) Olek ↑{grabs glue bottle}
343	SG:	I have one
344	G:	oh okay
345	S:	{goes through her pile to find some glue}
346	G:	I have to dig to through the bottom
347	S:	yeah
348	SG:	you can use mine ((0.5)) you can use mine
349	TA:	oh you want a glue stick↑ {leaves to get glue} ((3.2)) here Genie
350	":	{give her a glue stick}
351	AH:	I have a glue stick
352	G:	oh that's fine I have one
353	S:	yeah
354	G:	perfect
355	AH:	do we have to glue these on↑ {pointing to the paper}
356	TA:	yeah when you get em all cut out then glue this paper and then
357	":	Genie's gonna take them to her office and cover them in plastic

358	AH:	oh
359	TA:	{speaking to Genie showing her crafts} yeah cause the boys have
360	":	uhm when they're like this {displaying the crafts} they the three and
361	":	put em like a tree ornament
362	G:	yeah ((2.2)) I gave em five cause they color so fast
363	TA:	I see {nodding her head laughing}
364	G:	{laughing}
365	TA:	you get it all glued on Kalvin↑ {walking over to him}
366	K:	{nodding his head} ((5.6))
367	TA:	Monica
368	M:	{looks at the TA}
369	TA:	{puts her crafts in front of her} color ((4.0))
370	SG:	look at ((unclear)) {holding a container for the instructor to see}
371	G:	oh good girl
372	SG:	what's in this anyways↑
373	G:	clay ((2.2)) I just needed the circle ((4.8))
374	AH:	you can ((unclear))
375	SG:	not ((unclear))
376	TA:	okay go on Aleks and I'll help you{sitting down on desk}((4.0))
377	":	do we need another circle for this one↑ {leaning over to talk to Genie}
378	G:	yeah
379	TA:	like you did there↑use the bottom↑{grabbing margarine container}
380	G:	yeah {to the student as she finishes gluing the craft} there you go
381	S:	it spilled
382	G:	oh you're swift uhmm hold on
383	S:	quite splashing it
384	G:	let me back off {gets out of chair}okay Anna you finish the rest of
385	":	those but you don't cut it off you just put your name on those okay
386	A:	okay
387	G:	hey way to go one two three four we're missing one

388	S:	((2.1)) missing one another one
389	G:	yeah {walking together to the front} you're supposed to have five
390	S:	here's another one
391	G:	oh ho good stuff
392	TA:	okay Aleks look what I'm going to do
393	G:	are you going to paste it
394	S:	do we need to
395	G:	yes a glue stick
396	TA:	out
397	G:	go ahead {to a student} oh that's fine that's a fine circle just glue it
398	AH:	on and this one should go in the middle {to the TA}
399	TA:	yeah
400	G:	well were trying to cut some of our circles out so we're going to
401	":	make a new one
402	SB:	uh huh
403	G:	all you do is trace this put glue on the back of this one and then we
404	":	need to fix this one too
405	AH:	Allan left
406	TA:	no he's over by Genie
407	G:	Allan is right here okay this one needs to go in a circle and more for that one
408	TA:	okay when Genie puts the plastic on she can cut along this line okay↑
409	AH:	I don't want to ((unclear))
410	G:	no more scissors
411	G:	we need to clean up around our spots ((0.6)) because it is time for me
412	":	to go already
413	S:	{groans}
414	G:	great
415	TA:	can you glue these on fast
416	AH:	yeah
417	TA:	okay we gotta be fast

418   Ss: {start cleaning up}
419   Lesson is over

Appendix F

Skidegate 1st grade complete Haida lesson

01 U: head and shoulders {camera panning to individual students}

02 ": *skaaji xil 7ud* {touching their head and neck}

03 ": *kun 7ud xyaay* {touching their chest and arms}

04 ": *kun 7ud xyaay* {touching their chest and arms}

05 ": *kun 7ud xyaay* {touching their chest and arms}

06 ": *skaajii xil 7ud kun 7ud xyaay* {touching head, neck, chest and arms}

07 ": *skwaay kwaay 7ud stl'aay* {touching their back, hips, feet, & hands}

08 ": *sk'yaa'jii til 7ud skul 7ud kyaal* {touching their eyebrows, thighs,

09 ": shoulders and legs}

10 ": *skul 7ud kyaal* {touching their shoulders and legs}

11 ": *skul 7ud kyaal* {touching their shoulders and legs}

12 ": *sk'yaa'jii til 7ud skul 7ud kyaal* {touching their eyebrows, thighs,

13 ": shoulders,and legs}

14 ": *kul kun 7ud gyuu 7ud dul* {touching forehead, nose, ear and stomach}

15 ": *xangii kuugaa* {touching their eyes and heart}

16 ": *tsing 7ud hlk'aay* {touching their teeth and chin}

17 ": *tsing 7ud hlk'aay* {touching their teeth and chin}

18 ": *tsing 7ud hlk'aay* {touching their teeth and chin}

19 ": *xangii kuugaa tsing 7ud hlk'aay* {touch their eyes, heart, teeth, & chin}

20 ": *kuuluu skil 7ud* {touching their knees and belly button}

21 ": *xiihlii 7ud tlaats* {touching their mouth and top of their head}

22 ": *xaanga hlt'aa xuujii dogwul guudaa* {touching eyelashes side of body

23 ": and lips}

24 ": *dogwul guudaa* {touching their side and lips}

25 ": *dogwul guudaa* {touching their side and lips}

26 ": *xaanga hlt'aa xuujii dogwul guudaa* {touching eyelashes side & lips}

27 ": *kun kuntsii xul xiljii 7ud hluu* {indicating front, touching their nostrils,

28 ": back of their neck and indicating their whole body}

29 Ss: {boisterous and laughing} ((12.3))

30 G: okay uhh *gaaw uu hlaa* (sit)

31 Ss: {still laughing as they sit down}

32 G: okay uhh *gaaxaa hlaa* (stand)

33 Ss: {students stand up}

34 G: *gaaw uu hlaa* (sit)

35 Ss: {students sit down}

36 G: *gaaxaa hlaa* (stand)

37 Ss: {students stand up}

38 G: *kunjuu* (sneeze)

39 Ss: atchoo {pretend to sneeze}

40 G: *gaaw uu hlaa* (sit)

41 Ss: {children sit down}

42 G: *gaaxaa hlaa* (stand)

43 Ss: {students stand up}

44 G: *ƙaa ƙaa* (walk)

45 Ss: {pretend to walk in place}

46 G: ((unclear))

47 S: {repeat unclear}

48 G: stop

48 S: stop

50 G: ((unclear))

51 SB: can we play simon says↑

52 ((break in the taping))

53 G: {speaking to camera} on the flash card we have a picture of the object

54 ": on here and underneath is the Haida word {holding up a card} and what I

55 ": do is I let the kids I turn them upside down {puts the card upside down on

56 ": the floor} so they can't see what it is that's there and the kids pick one

57 ": from the top and after they pick one ((0.8)) after everybody's had one in

58 ": the circle what I do is read the Haida name out to them and then we place

59	":	them all in the middle and I put them in rows of three or four and they
60	":	close their eyes and they take about three away and they have to memorize
61	":	which ones or they have to memorize I give them time to memorize the
62	":	cards and then uhmm I take about three they close their eyes I take about
63	":	three or four them and they have to tell me in Haida which ones are
64	":	missing ((3.2)) and I always take the easy cards out
65	SB:	not always
66	G:	{begins to put a card in front of each student-cards have a picture of a,
67	":	mosquito seal canoe seaweed fern seal's face skunk cabbage goose
68	":	fence orca star and tree} ((5.3))
69	Ss:	{sitting in a circle on the floor they begin looking at each picture}
70	":	{poor recording quality makes it too difficult to hear what children are
71	":	saying as they look at the pictures}((1:21))
72	S:	that should be ((unclear)) {looking at the pictures}
73	S:	go put it away
74	SG:	keep it there {to another student moving the picture}
75	Ss:	{studying and holding the pictures}
76	G:	okay where do we have our cards when we get them
77	SB:	in front of us
78	G:	((2.5)) where do your cards go when you get them↑
79	SB:	on the ground
80	G:	huh↑ are we ready↑
81	S1:	yeah
82	S2:	some of us aren't
83	G:	Krystyna ((1.2)) do you remember what you have↑
84	K:	{looking at the pictures} *guud* (eagle)
85	Ss:	{begin looking through their piles}
86	S:	*guud* (eagle) he forgot
87	G:	ahh we're supposed to be sitting on our bottoms ((1.2)) ahh Kamila
88	K:	((unclear))

89   G: *aangaa* (yes) Bobby↑

90   B: {looking but does not answer}

91   G: *Sgaanaa* (orca)

92   B: *sgaanaa*

93   S: ((unclear))

94   G: good {looking at the next student}

95   S: ((unclear))

96   G: good {looking at the next student}

97   SBH:((unclear))

98   G: good good stuff Tye now we are going to leave them in the middle

99   Ss: {children make noise and giggle}

100 G: {puts all the pictures in the middle} remember what these were↑

101 ":   do we have to shut our eyes↑

102 G: not yet

103 Ss: {beginning to shuffle and making lots of noise}

104 G: Shhh

105 Ss: we had a good look at these cards

106 G: we're all supposed to be sitting on our bottoms too I shouldn't have to be

107 ":   reminding you

108 S: ((unclear explanation of why they have moved up))

109 G: well why don't you guys move back about an inch that's about this much

110 Ss: {all move back a little bit as they laugh} ((10.9))

111 G: look at those cards

112 Ss: {begin to look at all the cards to see which ones were taken}

113 S: look at them

114 Ss: {laughing and looking at the cards}

115 G: we're supposed to be looking at them quietly

116 Ss: {become quieter} ((4.0))

117 G: okay now what do you have↑

118 Ss: *kud hlk'aat'aajii* (fence) *tsii kultaxun* (mosquito) *ngaal* (kelp)

119 ": *sgaanǥa* (orca) *tluu* (canoe) *kaayts'aaw* (star) *tluu* (canoe)

120 ": *hlguun* (skunk cabbage) *tsiinaa* (fish) *kinxan* (tree)

121 SBH: that's that hardest

122 G: okay close your eyes

123 SBH: that's the hardest

124 G: close your eyes

125 Ss: {some close their eyes and some put their heads toward their laps}

126 G: {takes the pictures and puts them up a desk near the blackboard} sit on

127 ": your bottoms ((4.5)) okay Katie can you find *ngaal*↑

128 KH: *ngaal* (kelp)

129 G: *aangaa* and can you tell us what a *ngaal* is↑

130 KH: ((3.2)) kelp

131 G: good girl and how do you say kelp in Haida↑

132 KH: *ngaal* (kelp)

134 Ss: *ngaal*

135 G: what else are we missing Leon↑

136 SB: *tsii kultaxun* (mosquito)

137 G: *aangaa* (yes) what's a *tsii kultaxun*↑

138 SB: uhm ((2.2)) mosquito

139 G: good and how do you say mosquito in Haida↑

140 SB: *tsii kultaxun*

141 G: what else are we missing↑

142 SGH: *kaats'aaw* (star)

143 G: *aangaa* (yes) just one and what's star in Haida↑

144 SGH *kaats'aaw* (star)

145 Ss: *kaats'aaw kaats'aaw*

146 G: good what else are we missing Bobby↑

147 B: *tluu* (canoe)

148 G: ahh ((1.5)) *gaam* (no) *tluu* (canoe) right here ((0.4)) ahh Robin ((2.3))

149 R: *tsii kultaxun* (mosquito)

150 G: *gaam* (no) *tsii kultaxun* right here Rory what are we missing↑

151 RH: {sits and stares at the instructor but does not answer}

152 Ss: ((3.2)) {some begin to laugh}

153 G: oh let's not laugh okay uhhm Jaymie

154 JH: {hands in the air} *hlguun* (skunk cabbage)

155 G: good what's *hlguun*↑

156 JH: skunk cabbage

157 G: and how do you say skunk cabbage in Haida↑

158 Ss: *hlguun*

159 JH: *hlguun*

160 G: *hlguun* good we are missing one more what are we missing Vinny↑

161 V: {looking at the picutres but gives no answer}

162 SB: I know

163 SB: I know what it is too

164 G: Cherrie↑

165 C: *sgaanaa* (orca)

166 G: ahh *gaam* (no) *sgaanaa* is right here we're missing one more

167 S: fence

168 G: what is the Haida name for fence↑

169 Ss: {look at her but no one answers}

170 G: *kud hlk'aat'aajii* (fence)

171 Ss: *kud hlk'aat'aajii*

172 G: *kud hlk'aat'aajii kud hlk'aat'aajii* okay now uhhm we are going to play

173 ":   our ((1.1)) our hide and seek game okay(((3.5)) close your eyes

174 Ss: {move around boisterously as they sit with their eyes closed}

175 G: okay we should be sitting on our bottoms that is about the fifth time I

176 ":   told you guys to be sitting on your bottoms

177 Ss: {still boisterous}

178 G: okay quietly or we keep you ((unclear))

179 ?:   shhh shhh

180 G: {collecting all the pictures} shh ((16.4)) okay Katie will you find me *kud*

181 ": *hlk'aat'aajii*↑ (fence)

182 KH: {gets up and finds a pile of pictures by the black board picks up the

183 ": picture of the fence and holds it up}

184 G: what did you find↑

185 KH: fence

186 G: *aangaa* (yes) how do you say it in Haida↑

187 KH: *kud hlk'aat'aajii* (fence)

188 G: good girl ((unclear)) uhhm Bobby can you find me *tluu*↑ (canoe)

189 B: {goes to find the picture of the canoe}

190 G: what did you find Bobby↑

191 B: *tluu*

192 G: good go back to your seat

193 B: {gives the instructor the picture and then sits down}

194 G: Ronnie can you find me *tsiinaa*↑ (fish)

195 RH: {goes and finds a picture with fish}

196 G: what did you find Ronnie↑

197 RH: *tsiinaa*

198 G: *aangaa* (yes) what is *tsiinaa*↑

199 RH: fish

200 G: good and how do you say fish in Haida?

201 RH: *tsiinnaa*

202 G: Adriela ((3.1)) can you find me *kaayts'aaw*↑ (star)

203 AH: {goes to find the star picture and stands there waiting for the question}

204 G: what did you find Adriela↑

205 AH: *kaayts'aaw* (star)

206 G: and what's a *kaayts'aaw*

207 AH: a star {standing in front of the class smiling}

208 G: good girl have a seat

209 AH: {gives the instructor the picture and then sits down}

210 G: uhhm Vince can you find me *xuud* ↑ (seal)

211 V: {goes and finds the picture of a seal}

212 G: what did you find Vince↑

213 V: *xuud*

214 G: and what is *xuud*↑

215 V: seal

216 G: and how do you say seal in Haida↑

217 V: *xuud*

218 G: uhhm ((3.4)) Robin can you find me *tsii kultaxun*↑ (mosquito)

219 N: {goes up and looks through the pictures}

220 G: what do you have↑

221 RH: *tsii kultaxun*

222 G: *aangaa* (yes) and what is *tsii kultaxun*↑

223 RH: mosquito

224 G: and how do you say mosquito in Haida↑

225 RH: *tsii kultaxun*

226 G: good bring it to me and go to your seat ((.04)) bring it to me

227 Ss: {begin to laugh and make too much noise to hear clearly} ((21.2))

228 G: Jenni an you find me *sgaanaa*↑ (killer whale)

229 J: {goes and finds the picture waits for the question}

230 G: *aangaa* (yes) what did you find Jessica↑

231 J: *sgaanaa*

232 G: and what's *sgaanaa*↑

233 J: killer whale

234 G: good and how do you say killer whale↑

235 J: *sgaanaa*

236 G: *aangaa* (yes) uhhmm ((5.0))

237 G: Kelsey can you find me *xuud* (seal)

238 K: {goes to the pile and find a picture of seal waits for the question}

239 G: what did you find Kelsey↑

240 K: {stands there smiling shyly} *xuud*

241 G: and what is a *xuud*↑

242 S: seal seal

243 K: seal

244 G: how do you say *seal*↑

245 K: *xuud*

246 G: good girl uhmm ((3.5)) *howaa* (thank you)

247 K: {gives the instructor the picture and then sits down}

248 G: Camila can you find *kinxan* ((2.1)) *kinxan* (tree)

249 CH: {goes to the pile and doesn't find the picture}((3.4))

250 G: *kinxan* (tree)

251 S: ((unclear comments))(5.0))

252 G: look at the cards ((unclear))

253 Ss: ((unclear))

254 G: *kinxan* (tree)

255 CH: {finally finds the right picture}

256 G: good girl what did you find?

257 G: ((3.4)) Kevin can you find me *ngaal* (kelp)

258 KH: {goes to the pile and picks up the picture of kelp and stands waiting

259 ":   for the question}

260 G: what did you find↑

261 KH: *ngaal* (kelp)

262 G: and what is that↑

263 KH: kelp

264 G: and how do you say kelp↑

265 KH: *ngaal*

266 G: good boy

267 KH: {gives the instructor the picture and then sits down}

268 G: Danny can you find me *hlguun*↑ (skunk cabbage)

269 DH: *hlguun* {goes to find the picture}

270 G: what do you find↑

271 DH: *hlguun*

272 G: and what is *hlguun*↑

273 DH: skunk cabbage

274 G: and how do you say skunk cabbage in Haida↑

275 DH: *hlguun*

276 G: Billy can you find me *tyaahl guun*↑ (swan)

277 B: {finds the picture for a swan}

278 G: what do you find↑

279 B: *tyaahl guun*

280 G: and what is *tyaahl guun*↑

281 B: a swan

282 G: and how do you say swan in Haida↑

283 B: *tyaahl guun*

284 G: good uhmm Travis *ts'aa 7uul*↑ (fern)

285 TH: {starts looking for the picture}

286 G: *ts'aa 7uul* ((sitttin on the board))

287 TH: ((7.0)) {finds the picture of a fern}

288 G: good what did you find↑

289 TH: *ts'aa 7uul*

290 G: and what is *ts'aa 7uul*↑

291 TH: fern

292 G: and how do you say fern in Haida↑

293 TH: *ts'aa 7uul*

294 G: good uhhm Frank can you find ((unclear))

295 FH: {goes and looks at the pictures then glances at the instructor}

296 G: what did you find↑

297 FH: {holds up the picture}

298 G: what did I ask you to find↑

299 FH: {stands there without answering}

300 G: what did I ask you to find↑

301 FH: {speaking too soft}

302 G: good and how do you say ((unclear)) in Haida↑

303 FH: {speaking too softly again to hear}

304 G: good boy way to go{walks out of the class} *haawaa* kids (lesson over)

Appendix G

Skidegate Kindergarten Lesson: 12/98

1	G:	can we *gaaxaa hlaa* (sit) in our seats please↑
2	S:	*gaaw uu hlaa* (stand)
3	G:	*gaaw uu hlaa*
4	SG:	I'll do this
5	SG:	I want <u>that</u> ((to another girl for a teddy bear))
6	SG:	I'll do this
7	G:	go *gaaw uu hlaa* (stand) everybody[
8	SG:	][<u>I want that</u>
9	G:	] please
10	SB:	go go go go go go go go go
11	G:	<u>Bonnie</u> in your seat
12	SB:	go go go go go go go go go
13	G:	Jacob in your desk or in your seat
14	SB:	go go go go go go go
15	S:	Bonnie in your <u>seat</u>
16	SB:	<u>Bonnie</u> in your seat
17	B:	{runs to her seat}
18	G:	((4.8)) are you guys going to join us↑ [{to the students}
19	":	{looking at the mainstream teacher and TA] are they doing
20	":	something for her↑ {pointing at the children}
21	TA:	no you better ((unclear))
22	G:	yeah come and
23	TA:	I think they can join you
24	G:	come and join me come and sit down here {pointing to the table}
25	L:	{motioning to the girls to join the group}
26	SB:	I'm making ((unclear)) {putting hands over eyes like binoculars}
27	G:	ah who sits here
28	S1:	me too {putting hands over eyes like binoculars}

29	S2:	Tyler
30	G:	Tyler come on sit here
31	T:	I posed to sit this same place
32	G:	Who sits here↑
33	SGs:	Brad
34	G:	Brad sit here Aleks in your seat over there
35	":	are you finished↑ {to students offscreen} finish it later
36	TA2:	come on ((let's go))
37	G:	Megan in your seat LONNIE LONNIE ((4.5)) {looking at Lonnie}
38	":	Lonnie I need you in your *howaa* Lonnie {walks to board} okay
39	":	now let's see if we remember a one oh wait wait wait
40	SB:	you can't get rid of the line
41	G:	I can't get rid of the line↑ {erasing the blackboard}
42	S:	how come
43	G:	oh no OKAY {draws an illustration on the board}
44	S:	a big floppy
45	G:	a big floppy what ↑
46	U:	CRAB
47	G:	oh not a crab
48	S:	*k'uustan* (crab)
49	G:	*aangaa k'uustan*
50	S:	*k'uustan* ↑
51	G:	GOOD
52	SG:	what is that↑
53	S1:	*k'uustan k'uustan k'uustan k'uustan k'uustan* (crab)
54	S2:	no you don't
55	S3:	*k'uustan k'uustan k'uustan k'uustan*
56	G:	see we have our *k'uustan* then we have our↑ {drawing a 2nd picture}
57	S1:	WOW
58	S2:	*daaws* (cat)

59	S3:	*ang ang ang ang ang*
60	SG1:	*k'uustan* (crab)
61	SG2:	*kulgaayuugwang* (butterfly)
62	S4:	*kulgaayuugwang*
63	G:	GOOD
64	S1:	*kulgaayuugwang*
65	S2:	((laughter))
66	G:	Mandy and Jodi you need to listen
67	S1:	*kulgaayuugwang*
68	S2:	*kulgaayuugwang*
69	S3:	*kulgaayuugwang*
70	G:	good
71	S1:	*kulgaayuugwang* (butterfly)
72	S2:	yeah
73	G:	and what about this one↑ {draws a third illustration}
74	S:	((ga ga))
75	U:	((too loud and indiscernible)) ((10.5))
76	S1:	{laughter}
77	SB:	uh oh.
78	S2:	*((SWANSA)) ((SWANSA))*
79	SG:	*((SWANSA))*
80	G:	a *((swansa))* we have a ↑
81	U:	*((swansa))*
82	G:	what's this called Angela↑
83	A:	{does not answer}
84	Ss:	*((SWANSA)) ((SWANSA)) ((SWANSA))*
85	G:	OHH {making a zipping motion across lips responding to noise}
86	Ss:	{begin to be quiet}
87	G:	uhm Green table what's this one↑ {looks at the back table and
88	":	points at the third illustration}

89	Ss:	((*swansa*))
90	G:	GREEN TABLE {looking to her right}
91	Ss:	((*swansa*))
92	G:	GREEN TABLE {looking at students directly in front of her}
93	Ss:	((*swansa*))
94	G:	{disoriented looking at the tables} ((1.9)) GREEN TABLE
95	":	{motioning to students to her left the group at the green table}
96	GT:	((*swansa*))
97	G:	Yellowtable↑ {motioning to students and pointing at first illustration}
98	YT:	((*swansa*))
99	G:	HHH {gasping}
100	S:	*k'uustan* (crab)
101	G:	good what is it↑
102	Ss:	*k'uustan*
103	G:	and purple table↑
104	PT:	*kulgaayuugwang* (butterfly)
105	G:	good and this one is a↑ ((3.4)) *xuud*
106	S1:	*xuud* (seal)
107	S2:	*xaa* (dog)
108	S3:	*xaa*
109	S4:	*xaa* (dog)
110	S5:	*xaa*
111	G:	really ↑
112	S1:	*xaa*
113	S2:	*xaa*
114	G:	and what about this one↑
115	S1:	*daaws* (cat)
116	S2:	*daaws*
117	G:	*daaws*
118	S:	*daaws daaws daaws daaws daaws daaws*

119	G:	good and what about this one↑
120	S:	it's my cat hah hah
121	G:	what about this one↑
122	S1:	I like I love showing off
123	S2:	it's a shrimp
124	G:	oh what's its Haida name↑ {drawing a last image}
125	S1:	teacher
126	S2:	((*guudgaagilgaayd*)) (shrimp)
127	S3:	((laughter))
128	G:	what's this guy's Haida name↑
129	S:	((*guudgaagilgaayd*))
130	Ss:	((laughter))
131	G:	what's this one's Haida name↑ {pointing at the last illustration}
132	":	Karl and Inez sit in your seats
133	S1:	*guudgaagilgaayd* (shrimp)
134	S2:	*guudgaagilgaayd*
135	G:	*guudgaagilgaayd* good let's count *hala kwaayindaa*
136	S:	*guudgaagilgaayd*
137	U:	*sgwaansing* (one) *sding* (two) *hlguunuhl* (three) *sdansing* (four)
138	":	*tlayhl* (five) *tlguunuhl* (six) *jiiguugaa* (seven)
139	G:	oh let's start over {making a waving motion with her hand}
140	":	repeat after me *sgwaansing* (one) {holding up one finger}
141	U:	*sgwaansing*
142	G:	*sding* (two) { holding up two fingers}
143	U:	*sding*
144	G:	*hlguunuhl* (three) { holding up three fingers}
145	U:	*hlguunuhl*
146	G:	*sdansing* (four) { holding up four fingers}
147	S:	*sdansing*
148	G:	*tlayhl* (five) { holding up five fingers}

149	U:	*tlayhl*
150	G:	*tlguunuhl* (six) { holding up six fingers}
151	U:	*tlguunuhl*
152	G:	*jiiguugaa* (seven) { holding up seven fingers}
153	U:	*jiiguugaa* (seven)
154	G:	*sdangsingxaa* (eight) { holding up eight fingers}
155	U:	*sdangsingxaa*
156	G:	*tlaahl gwii swaansing gaw* (nine) { holding up nine fingers}
157	S:	*tlaahl (ten)*
158	G:	ohh *tlaahlgwii sgwangsing gaw* (nine)
159	S1:	I just said that
160	S2:	*tlaahlgwii sgwsangsing gaw* (nine)
161	S3:	(Jacob) said that
162	G:	*tlaahl* (ten) { holding up ten fingers}
163	U:	*tlaahl*
164	G:	good everybody at the purple table go find a place at the edge of
165	":	the green carpet
166	Ss:	{purple table students go to the corner}
167	":	oh are you at the purple table↑ {to a student at a different table trying
168	":	to go to the carpet}
169	SG:	{shakes her head and moves back to her seat}
170	L:	you guys are missing it
171	S1:	no
172	S2:	no you're not
173	S3:	I am
174	G:	everyone at the green table
175	Ss:	{green table students go to the corner}
176	S:	can I be green table↑
177	S:	no you're yellow
178	G:	and everybody at the {looking around} ((1.2)) [

179   S:] yellow table

180   G: yellow table

181   Ss: {yellow table students already walking to the corner}

182   G: come in Jane <u>oh</u> I'm so glad some of us know where the edge carpet is

183   ":   *gaaw uu hlaa gaaw uu hlaa* (sit down) ((4.5))

184   Ss: {finding a seat on the edge of the carpet}

185   G: come on *gaaw uu hlaa*

186   SB: jumping (box)

187   G: OH <u>*gaaw uu hlaa gaaw uu hlaa*</u> (sit sit)

188   S: ((laughter))

189   G: <u>Lisa Anne</u>   <u>Sonny</u>   are we ready↑

190   SG: yeah

191   U: *kaajii xil 7ud kun 7ud xyaay* {touching head, neck, chest and arms}

192   ":   *kun 7ud xyaay* {touching their chest and arms}

193   ":   *kun 7ud xyaay* {touching their chest and arms}

194   ":   *kaajii xil 7ud kun 7ud xyaay* {touching head, neck, chest and arms}

195   G: {walking off screen to a student}

196   ":   *skwaay kwaay 7ud stl'aay* {touching their back, hips, feet, and hands}

197   G: {walking to her spot stepping on a student' foot} sorry Basia ((ka)) uhmm

198   Ss: {student laughter}

199   ":   *xangii kuugaa tsing 7ud hlk'aay* {touching eyes, heart, teeth and chin}

200   ":   *tsing 7ud hlk'aay* {touching their teeth and chin}

201   ":   *tsing 7ud hlk'aa* {touching their teeth and chin}

202   ":   *xangii kuugaa tsing 7ud hlk'aay* {touching eyes, heart, teeth and chin}

203   ":   *kuuluu skil 7ud* {touching their knees and belly button}

204   ":   *xiihlii 7ud tlaats* {touching their mouth and top of the head}

205   ": *xaanga hlt'aa xuujii dogwul guudaa* {touching eyelashes, side, and lips}

206   ":   *dogwul guudaa* {touching their side and lips}

207   ":   *dogwul guudaa* {touching their side and lips}

208	":	*xaanga hlt'aa xuujii dogwul guudaa* {touching eyelashes, side and lips}
209	":	*kun kuntsii xul xiljii 7ud hluu* {touching their fronts, nostrils, behind
210	":	the neck and whole body}
211	G:	good *k'uuluu hlaa tlu yaadjuu* (touch your knees)
212	SG:	{touches her knees}
213	G:	{looking at and speaking to the girl} <u>good</u>
214	U:	{touch their knees}
215	G:	*skul hlaa tlu yaadjuu* (touch your shoulder)
216	Ss:	{some touching their head others touching their shoulders}
217	G:	{standing straight} ahh *skul hlaa tlu yaadjuu* {touching her shoulders}
218	U:	{touch their shoulders}
219	SB:	that's what I did
220	G:	*skwaay hlaa tlu yaadjuu* (touch your back) {touches her back}
221	Ss:	{touch their backs}
222	G:	Justine I want you in here {to a girl off screen}
223	SB:	good
224	G:	*skwaay hlaa tlu yaadjuu* {touches her back}
225	G:	come and stand right here {pointing to left} between Regan and Skyler
226	Ju:	{goes to the location}
227	G:	good ahh *staay hlaa tlu yaadjuu* [{touches her feet/toes}
228	Ss:	]{touch their toes}
229	G:	*k'uuluu hlaa tlu yaadjuu* [{slight pause then touching her knees}
230	Ss:	] {touch their knees}
231	G:	*kun* [{touching her chest} *hlaa tlu yaadjuu*
232	Ss:	]{touch their chest}
233	G:	*xiihlii hlaa tlu yaadjuu* [{touches her mouth }
234	Ss:	]{touch their mouth}
235	G:	*gyuu* [{touches her ear } *hlaa tlu yaadjuu* (touch your ears)
236	Ss:	]{touch their ears}
237	G:	*xangii* [{touches her eyes} *hlaa tlu yaadjuu* (touch your eyes)

238 Ss:]{touch their eyes}

239 G: *hlk'aay* [{touches her chin} *hlaa tlu yaadjuu* (touch your chin)

240 Ss:] {touch their chin}

241 G: *tsing* [{touches her teeth} *hlaa tlu yaadjuu* (touch your teeth)

242 Ss:] {touch their teeth}

243 G: *sk'yaajii* [{touches her eyebrows} *hlaa tlu yaadjuu* (touch your

244 eyebrows)

245 Ss:]{touch their eyebrows}

246 G: what is your *sk'yaajii*↑ (eyebrows)

247 SB: eyes

248 SB: *xangii* (eyes)

249 G: your what↑ {walking towards the children holding her eyebrows}

250 S: eyebrows

251 SB: *xangii* (eyes)

252 G: eyebrows good *kuul hlaa tlu yaadjuu* {touch your forehead}

253 SB: {touches his forehead}

254 G: *kuul* good *kuul* [{touches her forehead}

255 Ss:]{touch their foreheads }

256 SB: let me do it

257 G: *tlaats* [{touches top of head} *hlaa tlu yaadjuu* this area over here

258 S:]{touch the tops of their heads}

259 G:*hlk'aay hlaa tlu yaadjuu*(touch your chin){shaking her head at student}

260 ": hands to yourself please

261 Ss: {touch their chin}

262 G: *skwaay hlaa tlu yaadjuu* [(touch your back) {touches her back}

263 Ss:] {touch their back}

264 G: *skwaay* I 'd like Aleks and Chrisy to get to the edge of the carpet

265 A&C: {move to the edge of the carpet}

266 G: that way we will all have room same with Rufus

267 R: {moves to the edge of the carpet}

268	G:	okay let's *Xaa* (walk) on the spot [{starts walking in place}
269	Ss:	] {start walking in place} ((3.2))
270	G:	everbody *kaataas* (jump) { starts jumping}
271	S:	๏oohh
272	Ss:	{start jumping}
273	G:	*kunjuu* [{pretends to sneeze}
274	Ss:	]{pretend to sneeze}
275	SB:	*kunjuu* (sneeze)
276	G:	*xyaahl* (dance) ((0.5)) [{starts dancing}
277	Ss:	]{laugh and start to dance}
278	G:	*xyaahl* {continues dancing}
279	S:	{dance along with the teacher}
280	G:	*gaataa* (swim) Ronnie
281	Ss:	{pretend to swim}
282	G:	{pretends to swim} ((4.6)) ((*taay*)) [
283	TA2:	]good okay I'll talk to you later bye
284	G:	*t'aawiilgii* [{pretends to brush teeth)
285	TA2:	bye
286	Ss:	]{pretend to brush teeth}
287	G:	*taaynswa* (hum)
288	Ss:	{make a humming noise}
289	G:	*xaa xaa (walk walk)*
290	Ss:	{pretending to cough}
291	G:	{laughs as well turns around to look in the camera's direction} *xaa*
292	Ss:	{start walking in place}
293	G:	{starts walking in place} ((1.2))
294	TA2:	I in this totally slept morning I couldn't get up
295	S:	why don't we do ((*guusduu*))
296	G:	((unclear)) {starts running in place}
297	Ss:	{start running in place and lo}

298	G:	*xyaahl* [{starts dancing}
299	Ss:	] {start dancing}
300	G:	Ron Ronnie Ronnie {looking at him shaking her head VHS}
301	R:	why can't I
302	G:	okay watch me I want everybody's eyes over here and I want you to say
303	":	what I'm doing in Haida {starts dancing}
304	Ss:	*xyaahl* (dance)
305	G:	GOOD {jumps}
306	Ss:	((*kaatas*))
307	Ss:	((*kaatas*))
308	G:	{nods affirmatively and then starts walking}
309	Ss:	*xaa*
310	G:	{pretends to sneeze}
311	Ss:	*kunjuu*
312	G:	good let's do our *dup'juu 7ul'juu yang a jing* (tiny little spider)
313	SU:	*dup'juu* [
314	G:	] <u>no</u> ((3.2)) I want us to do it together
315	U:	*dup'juu 7ul'juu yang a jing* (tiny little spider)
316	":	went up the *gandl* (water) spout
317	":	down came the *daala* (rain)
318	":	and washed the *yang a jing* (spider)
319	":	out came the *xaaya* (bubbles)
320	":	and *gaagaa* (dry) all the *daala* (rain)
321	":	the *dup'juu 7ul'juu yang a jing* (little spider) went up the spout again
322	G:	good let's *hala kwaayi* [
323	S:	] I can do it <u>all</u> by myself
324	SG:	*hala kwaay indaa* (count)
325	G:	*hala kwaay indaa*
326	U:	*sgwaansing* (1) {showing fingers for each number} *sding* (2) *hlguunuhl*
327	":	(3) *sdangsing* (4) *tlayhl* (5) *tlguunuhl* (6) *jiiguugaa* (7)

328	":	*sdangsingxa* (8) *tlaahlgwii sgwaansing gaw* (9) *tlaahl* (10)
329	G:	good *gaaw uu hlaa* {grabs a chair}
330	S1:	*gaaw uu hlaa* (sit)
331	S2:	*gaaw uu hlaa*
332	G:	*gaaw uu hlaa* {leaves to the back of the room}
333	Ss:	((loud and restless))
334	S:	give me it
335	G:	((5:0)) {walking back to carpet} ((*haawohlaanaahluu*)) (be quiet)
336	Ss:	{immediately quiet down}
337	S1:	it's mine
338	S2:	teacher he called he called me stupid
339	G: OH we're not supposed to call anybody names ((2.5)) tell him you're sorry		
340	S1:	okay
341	S2:	look at the Christmas tree
342	G:	did I hear you say I'm sorry↑ {grabbing chair putting it beside her}
343	S:	Christmas tree
344	G: did somebody say I'm sorry↑((4.0)){looking around}did she say I'm		
345	sorry↑		
346	S1:	no
347	S2:	{shaking head affirmatively}
348	G: good and let's not do it again <u>and</u> we should have those here anyway		
349	": can I have it↑ {holding her hand out to wards the student} you shouldn't		
350	": of had them here anyways can I have them↑		
351	SB:	{stands up and give them to the instructor} ((3.4))
352	G: thank you {puts it on the table} ((2.4)) okay now I'm going to ask each of		
353	": you to name a number for me ((3.2)) Rufus are we listening↑ ((3.6)) ok		
354	S:	*sding* (two)
355	G:	nope {head shake} okay Krysia {holds up 10 fingers} *giisluu*↑
356	K:	((*sdang*))
357	S:	((*sdang*))

358   G: *gaam* (no) ahh Tye *giisluu*↑ (how many) {holding up 10 fingers}

359   T: ((8.2)) *tlaahl* (ten)

360   G: *aanga* (yes) ahhm Eliza *giisluu*↑ {holding up 5 fingers}

361   E: uuhm ((1.2)) *tlaahl* (ten)

362   G: *gaam* (no) Sonny *giisluu*↑ (how many) {holding up 5 fingers}

363   Sy: {no answer}

364   G: ((8.0)) Ronnie *giisluu*↑ {looking at Ronnie holding up 5 fingers}

365   R: uhm ((inaudible)) ((4.4))

366   G: *gaam* (no) {shaking head} ahm Brad *giisluu*↑ {holding up 5 fingers}

367   B: ((4.1)) I don't know

368   G: look up here and try and count

369   B: ((5.5)) *tlayhl* (five)

370   G: oh how did you know that↑

371   B: ((3.2)) Jake

372   G: Jake you have to let him learn on his own

373   S: learning time this morning

374   G: uhmm Aleks *giisluu*↑ (how many){holding up fingers}

375   S: {starting to count out loud}

376   G: ah ah ah ah

377   A: *swansing*

378   G: *aanga* (yes) uhhm Inez *giisluu*↑ (how many) {holding up fingers}

379   I: ((8.2)) ahh *tlguunuhl* (six)

380   G: GOOD GIRL I LIKE THE WAY YOU DID THAT Rufus *giisluu*↑

381   ":   {holding up 8 fingers}

382   R: ((5.4)) *tlaahlgwii sgwaangsing gaw* (nine)

383   G: <u>oh good try</u> close the one before *tlaahlgwii sgwaangsing gaw*

384   S: ((unclear))

385   R: *sdangsangxaa* (nine)

386   G: good what is *sdangsingxaa*↑

387   SG: eight

388 G: good ahhm ((4.0)) Cyrus *giisluu*↑ (how many) {holding up fingers}

389 C: *giisluu*↑

390 G: *gaam*

391 C: aahhm ((6.5)) *sding* (two)

392 G: *aanga* ahhm Kodi Kodi I'm right here *giisluu*↑ {looking at boy in

393 ": front of her holding up both hands }

394 K: *giisluu*↑(how many)

395 G: *gaam* (no)

396 K: ((5.6)) *tlaahl* (ten)

397 G: *gaam* {shaking her head VHS} ((4.8)) watch me *sgwaansing* (one)

398 ": {puts up 1 finger} *sding* (two) {holding up 2 fingers} *hlguunuhl* (three)

399 ": {holding up three fingers} *sdansing* (four) {holding up four fingers}

400 *giisluu*↑

401 K: *tlayhl* (five)

402 G: good ahhm Jason *giisluu*↑ *sding* (two) {holding up two fingers}

403 Ja: ((4.1)) *sdangsingxaa* (eight)

404 G: *gaam* ahmm ((1.2)) Gwen *giisluu*↑ (how many)

405 Gw: ((4.0)) ((unclear))

406 G: *gaam* ((3.0)) try again you're on the right track keep going

407 Gw: ((9.0)) *tlaahlgwii sgwaansing gaw* (nine)

408 G: GOOD GIRL I LIKE THE WAY YOU DID THAT boy I like to see kids

409 ": {models counting} counting out to themselves ((1.2)) to get the answer

410 S1: ((3.5)) *Sding* (two)

411 S2: *Sding*

412 G: oh hold on

413 S1: *Sding* (two)

414 S2: *Sding*

415 S3: *((swansing))*

416 G: Allie *giisluu*↑ (how many)

417 A: {no answer}

418   G: ((5.5)) Allie {holding up her fingers}

419   A: what↑ {starts looking at other students}

420   S: ((7.5)) {in a whisper} ((*tlawi*))

421   G: right here {waving her fingers} I'm right here don't look at anybody else

422   S: *((swansing))*

423   A: ((5.4)) *sdansingxaa* (eight)

424   G: anybody *giisluu* ↑ (how many)

425   Ss: ((2.3)) *sdangsingxaa* (eight)

426   S: *sdangsingxaa*

427   G: oh let's have all eyes up here okay quit fidgeting Kristie to the edge of

428   ":   the carpet and sit on your bottoms ((1.2)) sit on your bottom

429   S: ((5.5)) I'm squished

430   G: sit on your bottom

431   Ss: {start laughing}

432   G: if you guys would sit at the edge of the carpet then you wouldn't be

433   ":   squished sit up Asia

434   S: ((5.2)) hey

435   G: <u>Ronnie</u> ((1.5)) we're waiting for Ronnie Kuba and Rufus

436   Ss: {move to the edge of the carpet}

437   G: *howaa* Ronnie ((5.3)) kay now I want all eyes up <u>here</u> <u>listen</u> and

438   ": <u>watch</u> ((2.3)) {holding ears} okay <u>listen</u> and <u>watch</u> are you all watching↑

439   Ss: yeah

440   G: I don't see everyone's eyes on <u>me</u>

441   Ss: {break into laughter}

442   G: Ala ((2.0)) Krysia ((3.3)) now watch cause a lot of you are getting stuck

443   ":on this {begins to put her hands in the air ready to model the numbers}

444   S: *sgwaansing* (one)

445   G: Kodi no just listen {tapping him on the head} ((2.5)) [*sgwaansing*

446   Ss:] *sgwaansing*

447   G: just listen ((2.8)) do you understand↑ listen and watch

448   S: {laughing} yeah

449   G: {whispering loudly} let's listen and watch ((2.0)) *sgwaansing sding*

450   ":   watch ((2.0)) *sgwaansing sding* (one two)

451   S: ((5.0)) {laughs}

452   G: *sgwaansing* (one) {holding up one finger}

453   ":   *sding* (two) { holding up two fingers}

454   ":   *thlunuhl* (three) { holding up three fingers}

455   ":   *sdansing* (four) { holding up four fingers}

456   ":   *tlayhl* (five) { holding up five fingers}

457   G: *tlguunuhl* (six) { holding up six fingers}

458   ":   *jiiguugaa* (seven) { holding up seven fingers}

459   ":   *sdangsingxaa* (eight) { holding up eight fingers}

460   ":   *tlaahl gwii swaansing gaw* (nine) { holding up nine fingers}

461   ":   *tlaahl* (ten) { holding up ten fingers}

462   ": I'm going to do it again ((2.0)) *sgwaansing* (one) {holding up 1finger}

463   ":   *sgwaansing* (one) {holding up one finger}

464   ":   *sding* (two) { holding up two fingers}

465   S: *sding* (two)

466   G: *thlunuhl* (three) { holding up three fingers}

467   ":   *sdansing* (four) { holding up four fingers}

468   ":   *tlayhl* (five) { holding up five fingers}

469   ":   *tlguunuhl* (six) { holding up six fingers}

470   ":   *jiiguugaa* (seven) { holding up seven fingers}

471   ":   *sdangsingxaa* (eight) { holding up eight fingers}

472   ":   *tlaahl gwii swaansing gaw* (nine) { holding up nine fingers}

473   ": *tlaahl* (ten) { holding up ten fingers} Ala I'd like you to pay attention

474   ":   ((3.4)) *sgwaansing* (one) {holding up one finger}

475   ":   *sding* (two) { holding up two fingers}

476   ":   *thlunuhl* (three) { holding up three fingers}

477   ":   *sdansing* (four) { holding up four fingers}

478	":	*tlayhl* (five) { holding up five fingers}
479	":	*tlguunuhl* (six) { holding up six fingers}
480	":	*jiiguugaa* (seven) { holding up seven fingers}
481	":	*sdangsingxaa* (eight) { holding up eight fingers}
482	":	*tlaahl gwii swaansing gaw* (nine) { holding up nine fingers}
483	":	*tlaahl* {holding up 10 fingers} now you can all do it with me ((1.0))
484	":	now wait for me I say it first you repeat after *sgwaansing* (one)
485	":	{holding up one finger}
486	S:	*sgwansing* (one)
487	G:	*sgwansing*
488	U:	*sgwaansing*
489	G:	*sding* (two) { holding up two fingers}
490	U:	*sding* (two)
491	G:	{touching girl on her right on the head} you are not saying with us
492	G:	*sgwaansing* (one) {holding up one finger}
493	U:	*sgwaansing*
494	G:	*sding* (two) { holding up two fingers}
495	U:	*sding*
496	G:	*hlguunuhl* (three) { holding up three fingers}
497	U:	*hlguunuhl*
498	G:	*sdansing* (four) { holding up four fingers}
499	S:	*sdansing*
500	G:	*tlayhl* (five) { holding up five fingers}
501	U:	*tlayhl*
502	G:	*tlguunuhl* (six) { holding up six fingers}
503	U:	*tlguunuhl*
504	G:	*jiiguugaa* (seven) { holding up seven fingers}
505	U:	*jiiguugaa*
506	G:	*sdangsingxaa* (eight) { holding up eight fingers}
507	U:	*sdangsingxaa*

508   G: *tlaahl gwii swaansing gaw* (nine) { holding up nine fingers}

509   S: *tlaahl gwii swaansing gaw*

510   G: *tlaahl* (ten)

511   U: *tlaahl*

512   G: <u>good</u> now let's do the *dup'juu 7ul'juu yang a jing* once more

513   U: [*dup'juu 7ul'juu yang a jing* (tiny little spider)

514   G:] {performing song's motion for spider with her hands wiggling her fingers

515   ":   like a spider's leg }

516   U: [went up the *gondl* (water) spout

517   G:] {performing song's motion for spider moving upwards with her hands}

518   U: [down came the *daala* (rain)

519   G:] {performing the song's motion for pouring rain with her hands}

520   U: [and washed the *yang a jing* (spider)

521   G:] {performing the song's motion for washing spider away with her hands}

522   U: [out came the *xaaya* (sun)

523   G:] {performing the song's motion for the sun with her hands}

524   U: [and *gaagaa* (dried) all the *daala* (rain)

525   G:] {performing the song's motion for drying the rain with her hands }

526   U: [the *dup'juu 7ul'juu yang a jing* (little spider) went up the spout again

527   G:] {performing song's motion for spider moving upwards with her hands}

528   G: what's this called guy ↑ {performing song's motion for rain spider

529   ":   with her hands wiggling her fingers like a spider's leg}

530   Ss: *dup'juu 7ul'juu yang a jing* (tiny little spider)

531   G: good *dup'juu 7ul'juu yang a jin* what's this called↑ {performing

532   ":   rain motion with hands over head sprinkling motion downwards}

533   Ss: *daala* (rain)

534   G: good what's this called↑ {performing the song's motion for the

535   ":   sun with her hands rising in the air}

536   Ss: *xaaya* (sun)

537   G: uhhm what's this called↑ {performing song's motion for bubbling

538   ":   with her hands in a rolling motion}

539   S: *gaagaa* (bubbles)

540   G: oh what's this ↑ {performing song's motion for bubbles with hands}

541   S: *daala* (rain)

542   G: <u>no</u>

543   S: *gaagaa* (bubbles)

544   G: *gaagaa* <u>right</u> *gaagaa* everybody *gaagaa* {performing song's

545   ":   motion for bubbles again with her hands}

546   S: *gaagaa* (bubbles)

547   G: and what's this↑ {performing song's motion for rain with hands

548   ":   over her head then sprinkling motion downwards}

549   Ss: *daala* (rain)

550   G: everybody *daala* {performing song's motion for rain with hands

551   ":   over her head then sprinkling motion downwards} *daala*

552   Ss: {perform song's motion for rain with her hands over their head then

553   ":   a sprinkling motion downwards}

554   G: and *dup'juu 7ul'juu yang a jin* {performing song's motion for rain

555   ":   spider with her hands wiggling her fingers like a spider's leg}

556   Ss: {perform song's motion for rain spider with hands wiggling their

557   ":   fingers like a spider's leg}

558   G: good find your *k'uuluu* (knees)

559   Ss: {touch their knees}

560   G: good {touches her knees} *k'uuluu* find your *skul* (shoulders)

561   Ss: {touch their shoulders}

562   G: {touches her shoulders} good find your *kaajii* (head)

563   Ss: {touch their head}

564   G: {touches her head} find your *skil* (bellybutton)

565   SB: {gives something to the instructor}

566   Ss: {touch their belly button}

567   G: <u>good</u> {touches her belly button} some of us where their *skil* is

568	S:	I do
569	G:	what about your *xyaay* (arms)
570	Ss:	{waves her arms}
571	G:	oh no your *xyaay*
572	S:	{wait for her answer}
573	G:	your *xyaay* {running her hands down each arm} your *xyaay*
574	Ss:	{touch their arms}
575	G:	what about your *skwaay* (back)
576	Ss:	{touch their backs}
577	G:	good {touches her} and your *st'aay* your *st'aay* (feet)
578	Ss:	{touch their feet}
579	G:	*st'aay* {touches her feet} your *k'uuluu* (knees)
580	Ss:	{some touch their knees one touches his mouth}
581	G:	*k'uuluu* {emphatically touching her knees}
582	S:	*k'uuluu*
583	G:	your *k'uuluu* {touching her knees} pay attention
584	Ss:	{getting a little restless}
585	G:	you should be all on the edge of the carpet nobody should be bouncing
586	":	or moving around ((2.0)) your *k'uuluu* {touching her knees}
587	S:	*k'uuluu* (knees)
588	S:	Nathan
589	S:	do it Nathan
590	G:	{to boy on her immediate right} oh please tell her you're sorry please↑
591	":	((2.4))can you say sorry↑that's why we shouldn't be bouncing we should
592	":	be sitting like I ask ((1.8)) because you can hurt somebody ((2.1)) Ronnie
593	S:	Nathan ((unclear))
594	G:	Ronnie Ronnie Ronnie ((2.0)) you need to pay attention can we all *gaa xaa*
595	":	*gaaxaa hlaa* (stand) please
596	Ss:	{stand}
597	S:	ask me

598	G:	Ronnie *gaaxaa hlaa* (stand) please, good now one more time
599	U:	*skaajii xil 7ud kun 7ud xyaay* {touching head, neck, chest, arms}
600	":	*kun 7ud xyaay* (chest and arms)
601	":	*kun 7ud xyaay*
602	":	*skwaay kwaay 7ud st'aay 7ud stl'aay* (back, hips, feet and hands)
603	":	*sk'yaa'jii til 7ud skul 7ud kyaal* (eyebrows, thighs, shoulders and legs)
604	":	*skul 7ud kyaal* (shoulders and legs)
605	":	*skul 7ud kyaal*
606	":	*sk'yaa'jii til 7ud skul 7ud kyaal* (eyebrows, thighs, shoulders and legs)
607	":	*kul kun 7ud gyuu 7ud dul* (forehead, nose and ear and stomach)
608	":	*xangii kuugaa* (eyes, heart)
609	":	*tsing 7ud hlk'aay* (teeth and chin)
610	":	*tsing 7ud hlk'aay*
611	":	*xangii kuugaa tsing 7ud hlk'aay* (eyes, heart, teeth and chin)
612	":	*kuuluu skil 7ud* (knees, bellybutton and)
613	":	*xiihlii 7ud tlaats* (mouth and top of the head)
614	":	*xaanga hlt'aa xuujii dogwul guudaa* (eyelashes, side of body, lips)
615	":	*dogwul guudaa* (side of body, lips)
616	":	*dogwul guudaa* (side of body, lips
617	":	*xaanga hlt'aa xuujii dogwul guudaa* (eyelashes, side of body, lips)
618	":	*kun kuntsii xul xiljii 7ud hluu* (front of body, nostril, back of neck and body)
619	G:	you know what↑ when we are doing this you should be doing with me
620	":	((1.1)) otherwise you're not going to learn the parts ((1.0)) you understand
621	":	Ala↑ okay Asia you can get ready to go
622	A:	I go full day now
623	Ss:	{laughter}
624		.... (lesson is over)

References

Achneepineskum, Pearl. (1993). Charlie Wants. In Linda Jaine (Ed.), *Residential Schools: The stolen years* (pp. 1-2). Saskatoon: University Extension Press, Extension Division, University of Saskatchewan.

American Heritage College Dictionary. 3rd Ed. (1993). Boston, MA: Houghton Mifflin Company.

Andersen, Peggy. (2000). Washington High Schools go Native in foreign language instruction. *The Los Angeles Times*, Section B, Sunday, June 11.

Anker, D. E. (1975). Haida kinship semantics: 1900-1974. Duke University, Unpublished Ph.D. Dissertation.

Armstrong, J. C. (1987). Traditional indigenous education: A natural process. *Canadian Journal of Native Education, 14*(3), 14-19.

Asher, J. (1977). *Learning another language through actions: The complete teacher's guidebook.* Los Gatos, CA: Sky Oaks.

Ayoungman, Vivian. (1995). Native language renewal: Dispelling the myths, planning for the future. *The Bilingual Research Journal, 19*(1), 183-187.

Beals, Herbert. (1989). *Juan Perez on the northwest coast.* Portland, OR: Oregon Historical Society Press.

Beck, P.V., Walters, A.L., & Francisco, N. (1992). *The sacred: Ways of knowledge, sources of life.* Tsaile, AZ: Navajo Community College Press.

Bell, Rosa. (1993). Journeys. In Linda Jaine (Ed.), *Residential Schools: The stolen years* (pp. 8-16). Saskatoon: University Extension Press, Extension Division, University of Saskatchewan.

Blackman, Margaret B. (1982). *During my time: Florence Edenshaw Davidson, a Haida Woman.* Seattle: University of Washington Press; Vancouver: Douglas & McIntyre.

Boelscher, Marriane. (1989). *The curtain within: Haida Social and Mythical Discourse.* Vancouver: University of British Columbia Press.

Brandt, E. (1988). Applied linguistic anthropology and American Indian language renewal. *Human Organization, 47*(4), 322-329.

Browne, D. (1990). Learning styles and Native Americans. *Canadian Journal of Native Education, (17)*1, 23-35.

Campbell, G. (1990). *Compendium of the world's languages: Abaza to Lusatian. Volume I.* London: Routledge.

Cahill, T. (1993). Totems, tombs, and tall tales in Canada's Queen Charlottes: Adventure calls. *Islands, 6(*13), 94-105.

Cantoni, Gina P. (1999). Using TPR-Storytelling to Develop Fluency and Literacy in Native American Languages. In Jon Reyhner, Gina Cantoni, Robert N. St. Clair, and Evangeline Parsons Yazzie (Eds.), *Revitalizing Indigenous Languages* (pp. 53-58). Flagstaff, AZ: Northern Arizona University.

Celce-Murcia, M. & Larsen-Freeman, D. (1983). *The Grammar Book: An ESL/EFL Teacher's Course.* Rowley, MA: Newbury House.

Cleary, L. M. & Peacock, T.D. (1998). *Collected wisdom: American Indian education.* Boston: Allyn & Bacon.

Chiang, L. H. (1993). Beyond the language: Native Americans' nonverbal communication. Paper presented at the Annual Meeting of the Midwest Association of the Teachers of Educational Psychology. (23rd, Anderson, IN, October 1-2).

Cogo, Nora & Cogo, Robert. (1983). *Haida history.* Ketchikan, Alaska: Ketchikan Indian Corporation.

Collison, Art. (1993). Healing myself through our Haida traditional customs. In Linda Jaine (Ed.), *Residential Schools: The stolen years* (pp. 35-42). Saskatoon: University Extension Press, Extension Division, University of Saskatchewan.

Collison, William Henry. (1981). *In the wake of the war canoe.* Victoria, B.C.: Sono Nis Press.

Crago, Martha. (1992). Communicative interaction and second language acquisition: An Inuit example. *TESOL Quarterly, 26*(3), 487-505.

Cummins, Jim. (1986). Empowering minority students: A framework for intervention. *Harvard Educational Review, 56*(1), 18-36.

Cummins, J. (1991). Forked tongue: The politics of bilingual education, A critique. *The Canadian modern language review, 7(4)*, 786-793.

Dauenhauer, N. M. & Dauenhauer, R. (1998). Technical, emotional, and ideological issues in reversing language shift: examples from southeast Alaska. In L. A. Grenoble & L. J. Whaley (eds). *Endangered Languages: Current issues and future prospects* (pp. 57-98). Cambridge: Cambridge University Press.

Dawson, G. & Tolmie, F. (1884). *Comparative vocabularies of the Indian tribes of British Columbia, with a map illustrating distribution.* Montreal: Dawson Bros.

Diessner, R., & Walker, J.L. (1986). A cognitive view of the Yakima Indian student. *Journal of American Indian Education, 25*(2), 39-43.

Dorian, Nancy C. (1998). Western language ideologies and small –language prospects. In L. A. Grenoble & L. J. Whaley (eds). *Endangered Languages: Current issues and future prospects* (pp. 3-21). Cambridge: Cambridge University Press.

Dozier, Edward P. (1951). Two examples of linguistic acculturation : The Yaqui of Sonora and Arizona and the Tewa of New Mexico. *Language 32,* 146-157.

Dumont, R. (1972). Learning English and how to be silent: Studies in Sioux and Cherokee classrooms. In C. Cazden, V. John, & D.Hymes (Eds.), *Functions of language in the classroom* (pp. 349-365). Prospects Heights, IL: Waveland Press, Inc.

Duranti, A. (1985). Sociocultural dimensions of discourse. In T.A. Van Dijk (Ed.), *Handbook of discourse analysis* (V.1), (pp. 193-230). London: Academic Press.

Eastman, C. M. (1979a). Word order in Haida. *International Journal of American Linguistics 45*(2), 141-8.

Eastman, C. M. (1979b). Language reintroduction: Activity and outcome of language planning. *General Linguistics, 19*(3), 99-111.

Edwards, Elizabeth. (1982). The importance of pragmatic factors in Haida syntax. Ph. D. Dissertation, University of Washington.

Enrico, John J. (1980). Masset Haida phonology. University of California at Berkley, unpublished Ph. D. Dissertation.

Enrico, John. (1986). Word order, focus, and topic in Haida. *International Journal of American linguistics, 52(2),* 91-123.

Enrico, John, J. (1994). The Haida Dictionary. *Haida Laas 1*(8), 1,3 and 6.

Enrico, John J. (2005). *Haida Dictionary.* Fairbanks & Juneau AK: Alaska Native Language Center and Sealaska Heritage Foundation.

Enrico, J. & Stuart, W.B. (1996). *Northern Haida Songs.* Lincoln and London: University of Nebraska Press.

Erickson, Frederick. & Mohatt, Gerald V. (1982/88). Cultural organization of participation structures in two classrooms of Indian students. In G. Spindler (Ed.), *Doing the ethnography of schooling: Educational anthropology in action* (pp 132-174). Prospect Heights, IL: Waveland Press.

Feyereisen, P. & de Lannoy, J. D. (1991). *Gestures and speech: Psychological investigation.* Cambridge: Cambridge University Press.

Fishman, Joshua A. (1991). *Reversing Language Shift: Theoretical and Empirical Foundations of Assistance to Threatened languages.* Cleavedon: Multilingual Matters.

Fourth report of the standing committee on aboriginal affairs. (1990). *"You took my talk": Aboriginal literacy and empowerment.* Published under the authority of the House of Commons by the Queen's Printer for Canada.

Freeman, K., Stairs, A., Corbiere, E., & Lazore, D. (1995). Ojibwe, Mohawk, and Inuktitut Alive and Well? Issues of Identity, Ownership and Changes. *The Bilingual Research Journal, (19)*1, 39-69.

Friere, P. (1985). *The politics of education.* South Hadley, MA: Bergin and Garvey.

Friesen, V. Archibald, J. & Jack, R. (1992). *Creating Cultural awareness about First Nations: A workshop guide.* Vancouver: Native Indian Teachers Education Program, University of British Columbia.

Geological Survey of Canada. (1884). *Comparative vocabularies of the Indian tribes of British Columbia, with a map illustrating distribution,* by W. Fraser Tolmie and George M. Dawson. Montreal: Dawson Bros.

Greymorning, Steve. (1997). Going Beyond Words: The Arapaho Immersion Program Teaching Indigenous. In Jon Reyhner (Ed.), *Teaching Indigenous Languages* (pp 22-30). Flagstaff, AZ: Northern Arizona University Press.

Grenoble, Lenore A. & Whaley, Lindsey J. (Eds), (1998). *Endangered languages.* Cambridge: Cambridge University Press.

Haeberlin, Herman Karl. (1923). Notes on the composition of the verbal complex in Haida. *International Journal of American Linguistics 2,* 159-162.

Haig-Brown, Celia. (1994). *Taking control: Power and contradiction in First Nations adult education.* Vancouver: University of British Columbia Press.

Hale, K. (1998). On endangered languages and the importance of linguistic diversity. In L. A. Grenoble & L. J. Whaley (Eds), *Endangered Languages: Current issues and future prospects.* Cambridge: Cambridge University Press, pp.192-216.

Harrison, Charles C. (1895). *Haida grammar.* Edited by Alex. F. Chamberlain, Toronto: Copp-Clark.

Harrison, Charles C. Translator. (1898). *The Acts of the Apostles in Haida.* London: British Foreign Bible Society.

Harrison, Charles C. Translator. (1899). *The Gospel according to St. John in Haida.* London: British Foreign Bible Society.

Hayes, S. (1990). Education innovation at Lummi. *Journal of American Indian Education,* 29(3): 1-11.

Hirst, Lois A. & Slavik, Christy. (1990). Cooperative Approaches to Language Learning. In Jon Reyhner (Ed), *Effective Language Education Practices and*

Native Languages Survival (pp. 133-142). Choctaw, OK: Native American Language Issues.

Hymes, D. (1956). Na-Déné and positional analysis of categories. *American Anthropology, 58,* 624-38.

Jacobs, K. A. (1998). A chronology of Mohawk language instruction at Kahnawa:ke. In L. A. Grenoble & L. J. Whaley (Eds), *Endangered Languages: Current issues and future prospects* (pp. 117-123). Cambridge: Cambridge University Press.

John, V. (1972). Styles of learning-styles of teaching: Reflections on the education of Navajo children. In C. Cazden, V. John, & D. Hymes (Eds.), *Functions of language in the classroom* (pp.341-343). Prospects Heights, IL: Waveland Press, Inc.

Johnson, M. (1987). Canada's Queen Charlotte Islands: Homeland of the Haida. *National Geographic, 172*(1), 102-127.

Kaulback, B. (1984). Styles of learning among Native children: A review of the research. *Canadian Journal of Native Education, 11*(3), 27-37.

Kess, Joseph F. (1974). Pronominal systems in Haida. *Syesis, Volume 7,* 37-46.

Kirkness, V.J. (1998). *Aboriginal languages: A collection of talks and papers by Vera J. Kirkness.* Vancouver: V. J. Kirkness.

Kleinfield, J. (1972). *Effective teachers of Indian and Eskimo high school students.* Alaska: Center for Northern Educational Research, University of Alaska.

Krashen, S. (1982). *Principles and Practice in Second Language Acquisition.* Oxford: Pergamon Press.

Kroskrity, P. (1986). Ethnolinguistics and American Indian education: Native American language as a means of teaching. In J. Joe. (Ed.), *American Indian policy and cultural values: Conflict and accommodation* (pp.99-110). Los Angeles: AISC, UCLA.

Kroskrity, P. V. (2000). Language ideologies in the expression and representation of Arizona Tewa ethnic identity. In Paul V. Kroskrity (ed.), *Regimes of language: Ideologies, politics, and identities* (329-359). Sante Fe, NM: School of American Research Press.

Kwan, K. (1998). Bilingual education and the social context: A review of two context-oriented typologies. *Canadian Journal of Native Education, 9*(1), 3-21.

Labov, W. (1972). *Language in the inner-city: Studies in the Black English vernacular.* Philadelphia: University of Pennsylvania.

Lave, J. and Wenger, E. (1991). *Situated Learning: Legitimate Peripheral Participation.* Cambridge: Cambridge University Press.

Lawrence, E. and Leer, J. 1977. *Haida dictionary.* Alaska Native Language Center.

Leap, W. (1988). Applied linguistics and American Indian language renewal: Introductory comments. *Human organization, 47*(4), 283-291.

Leavitt, R. (1995). Language and cultural content in Native education. In M. Battiste (et al.), *First Nations education in Canada: The circle unfolds* (pp. 124-138). Vancouver: UBC Press.

LeBrasseur, M.M., & Freark, E.S. (1982). Touch a child-They are my people: Ways to teach American Indian children. *Journal of American Indian Education, 21*(3), 6-12.

Levine, R.D. (1977). The Skidegate dialect of Haida. Columbia University, unpublished Ph.D. dissertation.

Levine, R.D. (1979). Haida and Na-Dene: A new look at the evidence. *IJAL 45*(2), 157-70.

Lewis, Michael. (1997). *Implementing the Lexical Approach: Putting Theory into Practice.* Hove UK: Language Teaching Publications.

Lilliard, Charles. (1989). *The ghostland people: A documentary history of the Queen Charlotte Islands, 1859-1906.* Victoria, British Columbia: Sono Nis Press.

Lyovin, Anatole V. (1997). *An introduction to the languages of the world.* Oxford: Oxford University Press.

MacAvoy, J. and Sidles, C. (1991). The effects of language preference and multitrial presentation upon the free recall of Navajo children. *Journal of American Indian Education, 30(3),* 33-43.

Macias, K. (1989). American Indian academic success: The role of indigenous learning styles. *Journal of American Indian Education,* Special Edition, pp. 43-52.

Marashio, P. (1982). "Enlighten my mind. . . . .": Examining the learning process through Native American ways. *Journal of American Indian Education, 21*(2), 2-10.

McAlpine, L. & Taylor, D. M. (1993). Instructional preferences of Cree, Inuit, and Mohawk teachers. *Journal of American Indian Education, 33(1),* 1-20.

McAlpine, L., Eriks-Brophy, A., & Crago, M. (1996). Three teachers' beliefs: Issues from a Mohawk community. *Anthropology and Educational Quarterly, 27,* 390-413.

Mohatt, G.V. & Erickson, F. (1981). Cultural differences in teaching styles in an Odawa school: a sociolinguistic approach. *Culture and bilingual classroom* (pp. 105-119). Rowley, MA: Newbury House.

More, A. (1989). Native Indian learning styles: A review for researchers and teachers. *Journal of American Indian Education,* Special edition, pp.15-28.

National Indian Brotherhood. (1972). *Indian control of Indian education.* A policy paper presented to the Minister of Indian Affairs and Northern Development. Ottawa: National Indian Botherhood.

Ochs, Elinor. (1979). Transcription as theory. In E. Ochs & B. Schieffelin (Eds.), *Developmental Pragmatics* (pp.43-72). Cambridge: Cambridge University Press.

Ochs, Elinor. (1994). Human development, socialization, and language. Applied Linguistics Proseminar at UCLA, Winter and Spring quarters.

Palmer, Gary B. (1988). The language and culture approach in Coeur d'Alene language preservation project. *Human Organization, 47*(4), 307-317.

Pepper, F.C. & Henry, S. L. (1987). Social and cultural effects on Indian learning styles: Classroom implications. *Canadian Journal of Native Education, 14*(3), 54-61.

Peterson, Leighton C. (1997). Tuning in to Navajo: The Role of Radio in Native Language Maintenance. In Jon Reyhner (Ed.), *Teaching Indigenous Languages* (pp. 214-21). Flagstaff, AZ: Northern Arizona University.

Philips, S. (1972a). Acquisition of roles for appropriate speech usage. In R. D. Abrahams & R. C. Troike (Eds.), *Language and cultural diversity in American Education* (pp. 167-183). Englewood Cliffs, NJ: Prentice Hall.

Philips, S. (1972b). Participant structures and communicative competence: Warm Springs children in community and classroom. In C. Cazden, V. John, & D. Hymes (Eds.) *Functions of language in the classroom* (pp. 370-394). Prospects Heights, IL: Waveland Press, Inc.

Philips, S. (1983). *The invisible culture: Communication in classroom and community on the Warm Springs Indian reservation.* New York: Longman.

Philips, S. (1988). Similarities in North American Indian Groups' nonverbal behavior and their relation to early child development. In Regina Darnell and Michael K. Foster (Eds.), *Native North American interaction patterns* (pp.150-167). Hull, Quebec: Canadian Museum of Civilization.

Plank, G. (1994). What silence means for educators of American Indian children. *Journal of American Indian Education, (34)*2, 3-19.

Ramer, Manaster. (1996). Sapir's classifications: Haida and other Na-Dene languages. *Anthropological Linguistics, (38)2,* 179-215.

Report of the Assembly of First Nations language and literacy secretariat. (1992). *Towards rebirth of First Nations Languages.* Ottawa. Ontario.

Reyner, J.A. (1981). The self-determined curriculum: Indian teachers as cultural translators. *Journal of American Indian Education, (20)*1, 19-23.

Reyhner, J. and Rickey, Melissa J. (1991). Whole Language *NABE News, 15,* 2.

Rhodes, R. W. (1988). Holistic teaching/learning for Native American students. *Journal of American Indian Education, 27*(2), 21-29.

Ross, C.A. (1982). Brain hemispheric functions in the Native American. *Journal of American Indian Education, 23(3)*, 2-5.

Rowe, M. (1974). Relation of wait-time and rewards to the development language, logic and fate control: A. Part one: Wait time. *Journal of Research in Science Teaching, 11(2)*, 81-94.

Royal Commission On Aborignial Peoples. (1996). *People to people, nation to nation: Highlights from the report of the Royal Commission on Aboriginal Peoples.* Ottawa: Minister of Supply and Services Canada.

Sachs, Harvey. Schegloff, Emanuel A. & Jefferson, Gail. (1974). "A simplest systematics for the organization of turn taking in conversation." *Language, 50,* 696-735.

Sapir, E. (1915). The Na-dene languages. *American Anthropology, 17,* 535-558.

Sapir, E. (1923). The phonetics of Haida. *IJAL, 2,* 143-58.

Sawyer, D. (1990). Native learning styles: Shorthand for instructional adaptations? *Canadian Journal of Native Education, 18(1)*, 99-105.

Schumann, J.H. (1978). The acculturation model for second language acquisition. In R.C. Gingras (Ed.), *Second language acquisition and foreign language teaching* (pp. 27-50). Arlington, VA: Center for Applied Linguistics.

Seguin, M. (1988). Conversational completion in Sm'algyax. In Regina Darnell and Michael K. Foster (Eds.), *Native North American interaction patterns* (pp.143-149). Hull, Quebec: Canadian Museum of Civilization.

Shutiva, C. (1991). Creativity differences between reservation and urban American Indians. *Journal of American Indian Education, (31)*1, 33-52.

Sindell, P. S. (1974). Some discontinuities in the enculturation of Mistassini Cree children. In G. D. Spindler, (Ed.), *Education and cultural process: Toward an anthropology of education.* New York: Holt, Rhinehart, and Winston, Inc., pp. 333-341.

Spindler, G. & Spindler, L. (1982/88). Roger Harker and Schonhausen: From the familiar to the strange and back again. In G. Spindler, (Ed.), *Doing the ethnography of schooling: Educational anthropology in action* (pp. 20-46). Prospect Heights, Il.: Waveland Press.

Stairs, A. (1993). Learning processes and teaching roles in Native education: Cultural base and cultural brokerage. In K. McLeod (et al.), *Aboriginal languages and education: The Canadian experience* (pp. 85-101). Oakville, Ontario: Mosaic Press.

Stearns, Mary. (1981). *Haida culture in custody: The Masset Band.* Seattle: University of Washington Press.

Suino, J. (1988). And then I went to school. In R.R. Cocking & J.P. Mestre (Eds.), *Linguistic and cultural influences on learning mathematics* (pp.295-299). Hillsdale, NJ: Erlbaum.

Swanton, J.R. (1905a) *Contributions to the ethnology of the Haida.* New York: Leiden, E. J. Brill.

Swanton, J.R. (1905b). Haida texts and myths, Skidegate dialect. *BAE-B, 29.*

Swanton, J.R. (1908). Haida texts: Masset dialect. *AMNH-M 10,* 273-803.

Swanton, J.R. (1911). Haida. *HAIL I. BAE-B 40,* 205-82.

Swisher, K. (1990). Cooperative learning and the education of American Indian/Alaska Native students: A review of the literature and suggestions for implementation. *Journal of American Indian Education, 29*(1), 36-43.

Swisher, K. & Deyhle, D. (1989). The styles of learning are different, but the teaching is just the same: Suggestions for teachers of American Indian youth. *Journal of American Indian Education, Special edition,* pp. 1-14.

Tafoya, T. (1989). Coyote's eyes: Native cognition styles. *Journal of American Indian Education,* Special Edition, pp. 29-42.

Tobin, K. and Capie, W. (1980). The Effects of Teacher Wait Time and Questioning Quality on Middle School Science Achievement. *Journal of Research in Science Teaching, 17,* 469-475.

Toohey, K. & Allen, P. (1985). Domain analysis and second-language instruction in Northern Ontario Native communities. *The Canadian Modern Language Review, 41*(4), 652-668.

Toohey, K. & Hansen, P. (1985). Two contexts for training teachers of Native languages. *TESL Canada Journal, 2*(2), 11-28.

Van Der Brink, J.H. (1974). *The Haida Indians: Cultural change mainly between 1876-1970.* Leiden, Netherlands: E.J. Brill.

Walker, B., Dodd, J., & Bigelow, R. (1989). Learning preferences of capable American Indians of two tribes. *Journal of American Indian Education,* Special edition, pp. 63-71.

Wauters, J., Bruce, J., Black, D., & Hocker, P. (1989). Learning styles: A study of Alaska native and non-native students. *Journal of American Indian Education*, Special Ed., pp. 53-62.

Welsch, Robert J. (1975). Haida pronouns-Hydaburg dialect. *LEKTOS,* 118-134.

Whyte, K. (1986). Strategies for teaching Indian and Metis students. *Canadian Journal of Native Education, 13*(3), 1-20.

Wilcox, K. (1982/88). Ethnography as a methodology and its applications to the study of schooling: A review. In G. Spindler, (Ed.), *Doing the ethnography of schooling: Educational anthropology in action* (pp. 456-488). Prospect Heights, IL: Waveland Press, Inc.

Wilgosh, L. & Mulcahy, R. (1993). Cognitive education models of assessment, programming and instruction for Native learners. *Canadian Journal of Native Education, 20(1),* 129-135.

Wolcott, H. (1974). The teacher as enemy. in G. D. Spindler (Ed.), *Education and cultural process: Toward an anthropology of education* (pp. 411-425). New York: Holt, Rhinehart, and Winston, Inc.

Wolfson, Hannah. (2000). Tribes look to preschools to revive dying languages. *The Los Angeles Times*, Section B, Sunday June 11.

Yamuchi, L. A. & Tharp, R. G. (1995). Culturally compatible conversations in Native American classrooms. *Linguistics and Education, 7*(4), 349-267.

Index